HOW TO BECOME A SUCCESSFUL FINANCIAL CONSULTANT

HOW TO BECOME A SUCCESSFUL FINANCIAL CONSULTANT

Making a Living Investing Other People's Money

Jim H. Ainsworth, CPA, CFP, CLU

John Wiley & Sons

New York • Chichester • Brisbane • Toronto • Singapore • Weinheim

Copyright © 1997 by Jim Ainsworth
Published by John Wiley & Sons, Inc.

Library of Congress Cataloging-in-Publication Data:

Ainsworth, Jim H.
    How to become a successful financial consultant : making
a living investing other people's money / Jim Ainsworth.
      p. cm.
    Includes bibliographical references.
    ISBN 0-471-15561-6 (pbk. : alk. paper)
    1. Financial planners—United States. 2. Financial services
industry—United States. I. Title.
HG179.5.A373   1997
332.6'023'73—dc20   96-16259
                                      CIP

Printed in the United States of America

10 9 8 7 6 5 4 3

CONTENTS

HOW TO BECOME A SUCCESSFUL
FINANCIAL CONSULTANT

INTRODUCTION

I have been in the financial services industry for more than 30 years. That is an *honest* statement, but it is not what I call *forthcoming*. For purposes of this book, you can discount more than half of those years because I was not a financial planner—I was a CPA in public practice in a small town. I have been a true financial consultant and trainer of other consultants for only about 15 years. You can discount further because I didn't fully know what I was doing in financial planning for the first two or three years.

So why should you read a book about how to become a financial consultant by someone who has truly been a qualified financial planner (or financial consultant, whichever you prefer) for only a little more than a decade? For one reason: fifteen years as a qualified financial consultant puts me high on the seniority ladder in this business. There are many who can claim longer service, but few can truthfully say that they have been successfully running financial planning businesses for longer than that, mostly because of two factors. First, financial consulting hasn't been a profession that long. We're still learning how to be financial planners. We haven't even decided what we are going to call ourselves. Will we be financial planners, consultants, brokers, registered representatives, family financial counselors, financial advisors, investment representatives, or account executives when we grow up? Second, this is a rapidly growing profession and most of the entrants are new. The number of people holding the certified financial planner designation has soared to more than 30,000 in 1995, up by about 50 percent from 1990. I have held the designation since 1987.

A second reason you may find value in the following pages is that I have not been in the business long enough to have forgotten what it was like to enter it. I made many mistakes that I can help you to avoid. Thirdly, I believe that there are several ethical ways to enter this profession. I will discuss the merits of all of them without taking the position that only one way is the right way. A fourth reason is one that concerns me whenever I am reading an article or book. Does the author successfully practice what he or she preaches? Financial planning for others and taking my own advice have made me financially independent at age 51; the best part about this business is taking your own medicine. You use your own products, services, and knowledge to realize your own dreams.

The fifth and final reason for reading what I have to say comes from my background as a CPA first and financial planner second. I had the opportunity to conduct more than 10,000 interviews with clients over a period of 22 years. These interviews, for the most part, were in-depth and personal. Clients financially undressed in my office annually when I prepared their income-tax returns. I watched and monitored their progress from year to year. I kept notes on who was successful and who was not. I acquired invaluable information about their successes and failures and made discoveries about people and financial planning that I will share with you in these pages.

Financial planning is a terrific profession with a very bright future. This book takes a pragmatic approach in providing guidance to those who are attracted to the profession. We will not only explore the various routes to entering the profession but also frankly discuss how and why you get paid. We also give you the fundamentals of what financial consultants do and how to get connected to the right organizations and people in this business. You won't be a financial planner after reading the final chapter, but you should be able to decide whether you want to become one. You will also have a clear, step-by-step approach to meeting your career goals.

1

THE FORCES CREATING DEMAND FOR FINANCIAL PLANNING

Investment products and financial advice are changing dramatically from the way they have been offered for the past 50 years. This change is being fueled by (1) the necessary shift in the government's role in protecting its citizens from financial insecurity, (2) major increases in the number and types of financial assets that average consumers have available for investment, (3) the great boom in savings and wealth transfer that will be caused by demographics, (translation—baby boomers), (4) the abysmal savings rate in this country with generally poor preparation for retirement or emergencies, (5) technology, (6) the transfer of risk in retirement plans away from employers to employees, (7) the disappearance of financial windfalls from real estate—particularly personal residences, (8) and corporate downsizing. These eight factors will attract increasing media attention to the need for Americans to start planning their financial futures. An age of self-reliance is upon us.

Does this mean that we will evolve into a nation of do-it-yourself financial planners? How much training in financial planning does the average college graduate have? Most were never even exposed to the subject through 16 or more years of formal education. The majority of Americans will continue to need help. However, the media continue to place the profession at a skill and knowledge level just below ditch digging (using a shovel that has instructions written on the handle). Writers whose own financial affairs are a tangled mess will continue to advise Americans to do it themselves. Americans don't generally cut their own hair, do their own plumbing, or fix their own cars. Are most of them going to do their own financial planning? We were all given different genes and attributes. If one hates money matters and dealing with investments or insurance, one either gets help or gets in a mess. Most people have neither the time nor the inclination to do the things that are necessary to reach financial freedom. This natural diversity makes our economy work. We hire people to do things we don't want to do, can't do, or don't have time to do. Ninety-five percent of Americans will continue to fit one of those three descriptions. The demand for qualified financial planners will therefore continue to rise.

Much is being written and said about commissions versus fees today. However, the real substantive change taking place in the profession involves transaction-based business versus relationship-based financial planning. Doing business based on transactions will continue to be a lesser part of the market. We must now become real financial planners, which means creating financial plans. Again, this translates into tremendous opportunities for new entrants who approach the profession correctly.

THE CHANGING ROLE OF THE GOVERNMENT IN OUR FINANCIAL LIVES

For more than 50 years now, the government has taken on a larger and larger role in our financial lives. Dating back to the New Deal legislation that was designed to take us out of the Great Depression to the War on Poverty of the 1960s, government has fostered the idea that we can't and don't have to take care of ourselves financially. We now have two or three generations of Americans who think that the purpose of government is to provide for their needs. They believe that they are entitled to certain financial benefits from the government; these programs are even called entitlements. This thinking has spawned a group of politicians who willingly take on the role of the great providers. The system perpetuates itself because we do not have term limits and our elected representatives are willing to keep up the largesse in order to remain in office. This has led to the greatest deficit in American history. The deficit is increasing rapidly every minute of every hour of every day. Spending has to brought under control and entitlements must be curtailed. This is not a statement of opinion, it is a statement of fact. Americans must look to themselves more and to the government less for financial security. This new self-reliance, although painful at first, will force Americans to take stock of their finances and provide not only for their own basic necessities but for their goals and retirement. "Getting the government out of our hair" will increase the demand for financial services dramatically.

Current tax policies encourage consumption and discourage savings. Several pieces of legislation are currently proposed to change that. If a national sales tax is imposed, Americans will be taxed on what they spend, not on what they earn. Other versions of tax changes generally tax funds saved less than the current system or not at all. The American Dream IRA, if enacted, will encourage savings. The Kerry-Simpson proposal allows people to invest a portion of their contributions to Social Security outside of the regular Social Security system. I know that Congress has been all talk and no action when it comes to true reform of the tax system. When they have made changes, they were usually for the worse. They made things more complicated than ever. I made my living off the complexities of the tax code for more than 20 years. I believe we have a better chance of pulling it out by the roots now than ever before. It must be scrapped and I believe we now have the votes to force change. Whatever changes we are able to get should encourage savings and discourage consumption. Again, that translates into the need for financial planning advice.

We have been talking about the decline and fall of Social Security for many years. At first, politicians fed us various doublespeak and funny numbers about the trust fund and the future of Social Security. Now, virtually everyone agrees that the system cannot sustain itself when the large number of baby boomers starts to reach retirement. Since there is no savings build up for payment of future benefits, the system is not actuarially sound. The ratio of people paying into Social Security and those drawing out goes upside down starting in about 2011, when the first wave of boomers hits 65. In addition, we are experiencing much longer life spans today than when Social Security was enacted in the 1940s. People are drawing benefits longer and are taking out much more than they ever put in.

Raising taxes is not the answer. Social Security taxes are already higher than income taxes for most people. The retirement age has to be increased. Social Security might barely be available for the first of the baby boomers, but only if we have no recessions, continual economic growth, a rising birthrate, an increase in longevity of fewer than five years, and no dipping into the Social Security savings pot for the next 60 to 75 years. For many younger Americans, Social Security in its present form will simply not be available. People will have to provide for their own retirement, and they will need financial planning advice to do it properly.

INCREASES IN THE NUMBER AND TYPES OF FINANCIAL ASSETS AVAILABLE

When our parents were preparing for retirement in the 1950s, planning was simple. They didn't have that many choices. They hoped to see the value of their house increase, have a little money in the bank, and cut back on living expenses by staying home a lot and eating out of the garden. Ordinary Americans were not presented many choices. Most did not even know what a certificate of deposit was. Today, we have more than 5,000 choices in mutual funds with a smorgasbord of types. Individual securities are within the reach of many. Complex financial instruments are promoted at the bank, in the print media, over television and telephone, and on the Internet. More Americans than ever before look to financial assets to provide income in retirement and to reach their earlier financial goals. Can average Americans make sense of the current investment menu and make sensible choices to meet their needs? Although many publications are available for help in these areas, they usually focus on what is newsworthy rather than on what works for ordinary Americans. Also, most Americans have neither the time nor the inclination to digest the information from the various sources. In fact, many don't have the desire or ability to do it. The result is an increasing need for quality financial advisors.

MORE PEOPLE, MORE MONEY, MORE ADVICE

In his book *The Great Boom Ahead,* economist Harry Dent Jr. predicts an exciting new era of prosperity. This new era of prosperity is primarily caused by the baby boomers reaching their peak earning and spending years. They will also be inheriting the largest transfer of wealth in this nation's history. In his book *Age Wave,* Dr. Ken Dychtwald emphasizes that America is growing older. At the turn of the century, life expectancy was 47; today it is 75. This shift to an older population is a social inevitability offering challenges and opportunities for the financial planner. Dychtwald points out that many people may retire several times. "Since the shifting sands of money and assets in America are largely determined by the shape of the generational hourglass, how will a longer-lived society change the financial world of investments, pensions, mortgages, wills, and taxes? What will replace Social Security and Medicare, systems that depend on people dying at a younger age than they now are?"

How do these demographic changes relate to the demand for financial planning? Where will the clients of an aspiring financial consultant come from? I recently heard a speaker refer to several target market groups as Yuppies (Young Urban Professionals), MOOs (Married Only Once), DINKs (Double Income, No Kids), SINKs (Single Income, No Kids), and NIKEs (No Income Kids with Education). These are all cute acronyms, but I don't see an effective way for an aspiring financial planner to target these groups. The point is that demand for financial planning will be coming from many sources.

Everyone is talking about the boomers, so let's analyze their need for financial planners. The first ones will start retiring 14 years from now. Boomers with a median age of 43 have saved $103,000—just 11 percent of the $928,000 they will need according to an Equitable Nest Egg study. Two-thirds of boomers say planning for retirement is a top priority.

The group following the boomers is sometimes referred to as the no-name generation or Generation X. Do they need financial planning? They will almost certainly be forced to pay higher taxes to support Social Security payments for the boomers and will collect nothing for themselves from the Social Security system. According to a Kemper-Roper survey, 81 percent believe that Social Security will not be there for them. More planning will be required.

The pre-retiree age group ahead of the boomers owns more than 77 percent of all financial assets, yet has saved only 34 percent of the $843,000 they will need in retirement. As for the oldest age group of retired and elderly, they will be transferring trillions to their boomer children and grandchildren. They will need help in getting it transferred without the IRS taking a huge bite. They will also need help planning for long-term health care.

THE GREAT AMERICAN FINANCIAL DILEMMA

Americans do a lousy job of planning their finances. Approximately 95 percent of Americans reach age 65 at least partially dependent on Social Security; 85 percent are flat broke at retirement. Our net national savings is the lowest in the industrialized world. It was 7.7 percent of the gross national product (GNP) in 1980. It dropped 3 percent in the 1980s and is still dropping. The personal savings rate was 8 percent in the 1970s. In 1994 it was 4.1 percent.

How can this happen in one of the wealthiest countries on Earth? Many Americans have just given up. They don't have prosperity consciousness. They don't think they deserve to be wealthy or even financially independent. The government has been sending them the wrong message for decades. Savers and accumulators are penalized. During life, the government will do everything within its power to punish people for accumulating wealth. If people successfully fend it off during life, the government will be waiting with onerous death taxes. Previous bouts with inflation told people that money only decreases in value, so they should spend it. Many of my clients used to tell me that they had some money they needed to get rid of: "Let's get it out of the bank and put it where it can do me some good." They don't understand or believe in financial assets. Many would believe in the assets if they could only comprehend them. Americans don't understand how regular small investments over a long period can lead to financial independence. Although we shouldn't have to dodge the government's many bullets, good financial planning can do just that. However, the biggest market of all, average Americans don't see themselves as financial planning clients.

Even though I have given you lots of statistics about boomers and changing demographics to support the increasing demand for good financial consultants for many decades, I think there is a tremendous market being overlooked that would exist despite these favorable demographics. These are the people whose assets and income don't show up in surveys, because they are not asked to participate. They are not "target markets" for most financial planners and do not seek out consultants. Although some studies show that 75 percent of the population has never approached a financial planner, I think the percentage is much higher. The people who "suffer silently" don't participate in surveys. My best financial planning clients were found in this group. They are usually badly in need of help, willing to listen to you, and eager to follow a plan that you develop for them. Generally, they have not been hounded by product salespersons or burned in prior relationships with poor financial consultants. Best of all, they are grateful when a good financial planner helps them achieve their dreams.

TECHNOLOGY

This is truly the information age. With major advances in technology, it is possible for an average citizen to obtain current information that is mind-boggling in its sheer volume and timeliness. Information is available from so many sources in such quantity that consumers are confused about where and when to retrieve it and how to use it. They are being urged to get on the information superhighway before they are ready to drive. Media attention to this great information source has left average Americans feeling downright obsolete if they do not regularly "surf the net." Even if ordinary citizens had the computer capability to access the information, they could not possibly absorb it all.

Technology is not just causing information overload as a result of more people having computers—it is making information available to astute companies that feed it to us regularly through newspapers, television, radio, magazines, books, and the telephone. Even average people who don't own computers, or don't know how to use those they have, can't escape the bombardment of information. They feel the need to absorb it all and use it but are frustrated when they can't even begin the process. They need help.

Technology is affecting financial planning in other ways, also. The average financial consultant can now serve more clients in more ways than ever before. Computers enable a good financial planner to download information from many sources, sorting through the confusing array of facts and distilling them.

When I started implementing financial plans for clients, I was surprised at the lack of software to track client portfolios. Ordinary financial planners depending on their own resources were not able to deliver simple lists of all their clients' holdings. There wasn't a good system to show rates of return, tax basis, and so forth. Even the huge wirehouses turned out monthly statements to clients steeped in complexity and buzzwords or terms the average client or professional could not understand. The clients couldn't read them, CPAs couldn't read them, even many brokers didn't understand them well enough to explain the contents to clients.

I felt the urgent need to supply my clients with meaningful reports on their financial positions and progress toward their goals. It seemed like a simple problem that would be easy to solve with good accounting controls. I considered what I wanted to know about my own portfolio:

1. A complete list of all my holdings totaled by category of asset
2. Dates when I purchased these holdings
3. How well these holdings have performed since I purchased them

I also thought it would be nice to know my tax basis and current gain or loss position with each asset held. To my consternation, I found that I could not easily provide this information monthly to more than 50 clients. Why? Because the values of the holdings change daily. There was no source from which to download the information needed.

Cooperation was needed from both sides of the equation. The mutual fund companies had to be able to provide download capability and a software development firm had to be able to capture the information in a usable format. We were finally able to purchase software to download mutual fund prices and dividends, but then we had to call to obtain values for tax-deferred annuities and other holdings. When our business grew to more than 500 clients with more than 3,000 accounts, providing current information on a monthly basis became an administrative nightmare. Providing rates of return that were accurate was also next to impossible. When clients simply made an investment and kept it, we could easily calculate rates of return. When they did dollar cost averaging (regular investments of the same amount over a period) or periodically made random investments or withdrawals, the process became impossible. I wish I could say that today's technology brings this information to your fingertips. Unfortunately, it does not. However, it is vastly improved from where it was then. During the next five years, I expect giant leaps in this extremely important technological development, which translates to a greater ability to do good work for clients and to more opportunities in financial planning.

Today's financial planners can create customized financial plans specifically suited to their clients' needs. It is true that financial planning software has been around for a long time, but only recently has it offered more than one-size-fits-all solutions. Today, a good financial planner doesn't even need to purchase software. In fact, I recommend that beginning consultants use standard financial planning software cautiously (if at all) until they can prepare a plan without the use of software. Today's modular approaches to financial planning allow more flexibility than ever before, but it is still easy to fall into the trap of letting the software do the thinking. To truly serve the financial planning needs of individual clients, good financial consultants must take the holistic approach and design custom plans for their individual needs.

How did financial planners even function when they did not have financial planning software and were unable to provide meaningful information to their clients monthly? Some financial planners worked with only a few clients so that they could provide them with the service they needed and deserved. Some let the statements from clearing firms, their broker-dealers, and mutual fund companies suffice for reporting. When clients did not understand, good planners responded with explanations. Many simply kept working based on transactions rather than relationships. Old clients were ignored in the quest for new ones. Explanation of clients' current positions and the directions of their goals was secondary to finding the latest and best product. Brokers and planners were primarily paid based on the value of transactions they generated. In many offices, transactions were necessary for survival. There was no time to report to the client. Clients did not know any better, and many liked the fast-paced world of picking the best stock or bond. With today's tremendous knowledge base, clients demand more—and financial planners can deliver because of new technology.

THE TRANSFER OF RISK TO EMPLOYEES IN TODAY'S RETIREMENT PLANS

Only a few years ago, people took a common career path. They found a good job with a big company and worked there until they retired. When they retired, the company provided them with a fixed amount of income for the remainder of their lives. These types of company retirement plans were called *defined benefit plans.* Decisions about investments in the plans were made by the company. Employees generally did not know or care where the investments were made as long as the company agreed to provide the agreed-upon benefit at retirement. Employers made the investments and bore the risk. If investments inside the plan performed below expectations, then the employer had to make up the difference. Better-than-expected investment results meant fewer contributions had to be made to the plan. There was no risk for employees who happened to retire "in a down market." They knew what they were going to receive. Of course, the system wasn't perfect. There was always the risk of the company going bankrupt. Also, some companies abused the rules and squeezed out employees just before they qualified for full benefits. Enter the federal government. By the time it was finished writing rules and reporting requirements, it effectively killed defined benefit plans in the process of trying to protect workers. Today, defined benefit plans are the exception rather than the rule. Employers can no longer afford the onerous and expensive requirements.

Today, 52 percent of Americans are involved with a 401K plan. According to Access Research of Windsor, Connecticut, 401Ks are

39 percent of the total retirement planning market. Simplified employee pension plans and IRAs constitute an increasing share of the market as well. These plans transfer market and other risks to the employee. Most 401K contributions come primarily from the employee. The employer may match a portion or all of the employees' contributions, but most of the decisions about where funds are invested belong to the employee. Also, the employees' selections of retirement plan investment options directly affect the amount of their retirement nest eggs and incomes. Originally, employees were ill prepared to make such decisions. Without good advice, they put most of their funds in non-growth options that traditionally yield the lowest long-term returns. Also, if employees retired when interest rates or markets were down, their retirement funds were inadequate. As a result, many have been required to reduce their planned standard of living at retirement. Advising both employers and employees about proper asset allocation inside a retirement plan represents a tremendous opportunity for today's financial planner. Many planners also opt to get involved in setting up such plans, which creates opportunities for developing continuing client relationships with employees and employers. It can also provide a steady income stream.

THE DISAPPEARANCE OF FINANCIAL WINDFALLS FROM REAL ESTATE

Common investment advice when I was growing up was "buy land—they're not making any more of it." Fortunes have been made (and lost) in real estate. Most of these fortunes were not made by the typical man or woman on the street. However, average citizens did enjoy windfall profits by simply owning a home for the last three decades. Homeowners who bought in the 1950s, 1960s, 1970s, and even part of the 1980s generally enjoyed huge increases in the values of their homes. Many small fortunes were made by otherwise naive investors. They simply bought a home they liked and wanted to live in. Most did not forecast the large run-up in real estate values that took place in the 1980s. Many were able to take advantage of tax benefits on the sale of a home, buy a lesser home, and fund a significant portion of their retirement nest eggs. Many just kept trading up and deferring their gains into larger and larger houses. Although many huge increases in property values were reduced in the late 1980s and early 1990s, many investors are still sitting on huge profits. What does this mean to the demand for financial planning? First, many people still remember only recent history. They think that these large increases are going to be coming around again. However, demographics discussed earlier show that new home buyers will not be following the baby boomers. They are the first generation ever to be followed by a smaller generation. Finding alternate sources for funding retirement has always been important, but never more important than in the years ahead. Also, real estate owners will need advice on what to do with profits that have not disappeared.

CORPORATE DOWNSIZING

Corporate downsizing was once thought to be a temporary blip on the economic radar screen. It was thought to be fueled by greed, leveraged buyouts, junk bonds, and merger mania. That is one aspect, but it is also true that our country overflowed with bloated corporations full of bureaucrats. They resembled small governments with many people simply shuffling paper. Lean and mean is the forecast for the near, and I think distant, future. Technology is fueling much of this change, also. Smaller companies are making it tougher for large powerhouses to remain competitive in prices, services, or products.

Where do financial consultants fit in? People will be asked to take early retirement packages when the corporation starts to shrink. These packages usually involve lump-sum distributions accompanied by significant tax complications. How recipients handle these distributions will not only affect their current tax liabilities, but their entire postdistribution financial lives. Also, lean and mean corporations fuel the need for well-planned compensation packages for employees. There will be fewer of them, but they will be well paid and expected to attain high levels of performance. Compensation packages must be designed to keep employees from leaving without breaking the company. More and smaller corporations are potential financial planning clients for retirement plans, tax planning, financial planning as a fringe benefit, and so forth.

I have provided eight major reasons for an increase in demand for financial planning services. There are probably many others. Some may affect your personal goals and situation more than others. Still not convinced of the huge present and future demand for financial planning? Look around you. Are your friends in need of financial planning assistance? How about your family? Colleagues at work? You?

2

WHAT DOES A FINANCIAL PLANNER DO?

I said earlier that almost anyone can call himself or herself a financial planner. Insurance agents started using the term years ago. There are certain legal restrictions on the use of the term if you are a registered representative or a registered investment advisor, but they are so confusing that everyone has a different opinion as to when it is against the rules. Since financial planning is not a science and never will be, I doubt that we will ever be able to conclusively define who can call themselves financial planners and who cannot. Even if we do, what are we going to do with all the people who just start calling themselves investment advisors, family financial counselors, and so forth? I think that the *name* we put on what we do has some importance to get our message out to the public, but I do not think it is as important as *what we actually do*.

Financial consultants may work for salaries or may be entrepreneurs who have their own client bases. Financial planners may work for banks, insurance companies, or investment companies. They may be brokers for a wirehouse. They may be trainers with their own training companies. Financial consultants may work in the back offices or training divisions of broker-dealers. Many work for financial planning firms for a salary. A few may work in the corporate environment providing financial planning assistance to fellow employees. This book is written for the person who wants to be able to have his or her own financial planning firm. If you are capable of doing that, you can usually take that knowledge and apply it to the other opportunities described.

When asked what I do, I try to say that I help people achieve their fondest hopes, dreams, and aspirations. Sounds like a tall order, doesn't it? Also sounds like I may be overstating my abilities. All true, but I still believe that is what all financial planners should aspire to do. Many would say that people's hopes, dreams, and aspirations aren't about money and therefore have no connection to financial planning. I agree that many hopes and dreams are not about money, but most involve it either directly or indirectly.

In chapter 9, I discuss my discoveries about people and their money and the stages of mastery over money. I call stage 8 *Freedom* and stage 9, the final stage, *Freedom, Balance, and Generosity*. For most of us, reaching those stages is critical to achieving our dreams. It's important to enjoy the moment and live your dream on a day-to-day basis; however, most people don't discover that until they reach middle age or beyond. They keep running into house payments, medical bills, car repairs, and the other day-to-day things that keep us in a rut. It takes a strong mental state and an ironclad belief system to keep out of that rut when financial problems are ever present. Also, I don't believe that planning for the future is in conflict with living in and enjoying the present. In fact, I think they are wholly compatible. If you have someone to help you design a road map that leads toward your goals, it is much easier to get out of the rut and walk on the high ground.

A lot of hopes and dreams involve financial security and the ability to be generous with others. Can you be generous when you have no money? Certainly, you can be generous with yourself and your time. Money shouldn't matter, but, in fact, it does. Even the most spiritual among us can't ignore it. Even when money isn't important to us personally, it often fuels the engine of the organization that keeps our most altruistic dreams alive.

PSYCHOLOGY AND FINANCIAL PLANNING

Is financial planning all about money, then? I don't believe it is. I practice holistic financial planning. Many interpret that to mean the completion of a financial plan with all the textbook components for every client. It doesn't mean that to me. It means considering the whole person when you assist clients in planning their lives. It is true that your primary role may involve investments, insurance, taxes, and other financial matters, but you must be able to tie these things into the person's spirituality. You must be able to find out "where he lives." What things are important to him? Why are they important? How does she feel about herself? How does he feel about money? Does she have prosperity consciousness? Is he willing to be wealthy or financially secure? If not, why not? If you are working with a couple, how do they feel about each other? How do their goals work together? Conflict? Does it sound like psychological and people skills are more important than technical ones? I believe they are. You must be competent when it comes to financial planning, investments, and insurance, but technical knowledge is often secondary to interpersonal skills for really successful financial planners.

THE DESIRE TO SERVE

Don't let the psychological aspect scare you. You can learn how to find out what you need to know about people by mastering the skill of asking simple questions, listening, and recording the answers. You can be a great financial counselor if you apply common sense with a genuine desire to help other people. If you don't have that genuine desire but are motivated primarily by fees or commissions, I believe that you can change. You can learn how to be a caring person interested in the welfare of others by simply practicing that way of life. I know this because I have done it. I started in financial planning looking out for myself. Of course, I gave a lot of lip service to helping people meet their financial goals, but I was really in it for myself more than anything else. I certainly would not have done anything intentionally to hurt my clients, but I wasn't primarily driven by the desire to serve. I wanted my clients to be served well, but mostly because that worked to my benefit. When I realized this could be profitable but wasn't personally satisfying, I started thinking and acting as if I cared. Before long, I learned how to care more about my clients and thought almost nothing about the money I was going to make. That is when I started to be a good financial planner and to make more money than I ever thought possible.

THE PARABLE OF THE WHEEL

We now know that financial consultants help people achieve their goals and dreams. We know that to be quality financial planners who enjoy our work, we must learn to put service to others above all else. That sounds good on paper, but how do we apply it to real life? What do we actually do when sitting across the table from a client? Imagine the financial planning process as a huge wagon wheel. In the center or hub of the wheel is the client, who is tied with many different ropes to nine spokes in the wheel. Each strand of rope is of a different material. Each is of a different strength and durability. The spokes of the wheel are as follows:

1. Risk and insurance
2. Investments
3. Taxes
4. Education and other child-related expenses
5. Funds for emergencies, goals other than retirement, and cash flow planning
6. Retirement planning
7. Asset protection
8. Old age and elder care planning
9. Transfer planning

Transfer planning is substituted for estate planning or death planning. Most people don't believe they *have* an estate and they certainly don't want to plan their own *deaths*. They will, however, discuss transfer of their assets *away* from the IRS to their loved ones or to charity.

Now, the wheel and the client are in a long narrow rut or ditch. The rut is there to keep the client from completely falling down with his wheel and from rolling so fast that he loses control. The client can, with some effort, manage to roll the wheel as long as he stays in the rut. The sides of the rut serve to break his fall and slow him down. He is unable to leave the rut without losing control or falling down with the wheel. He is also dizzy from the constant rolling and tired from the weight of the wheel and from being tied up.

The Top of the Mountain

Now imagine that the rut goes all the way around a mountain. This is a huge mountain with winding trails leading in various directions, but only two or three lead to the top. The rest meander around the bottom and wind up at the same place where they started. The mountain has several plateaus representing the various stages of mastery over money. The top of the mountain is stage 9, representing the spirit of *Freedom, Balance, and Generosity.*

The job of a good financial planner is to give clients a tool to untie or cut each rope. Remember that they are made of various materials with various strengths and varying thicknesses. They are also tied with knots of varying degrees of tightness and complexity to untie. Some will be easy, others much more difficult. At least one of the knots is secured with a lock. The key to the lock is in the client's pocket, but he can't reach it. The client also knows how to untie some of the knots but doesn't have the information to fully free himself. The information inside the client's head (the key) must be combined with the financial consultant's information in order to free the client completely from the wheel. The financial planner must find the tools to untie each knot or cut each rope to free the client. The consultant must also convince the client to give him the key to the lock. The client can't ever leave the wheel but he should be able to maneuver it. When he is free from the wheel he will be able to stand on his own and roll it in any direction he chooses. He can use it to move large objects if he is able to stand on the ground. He may even build other wheels and create a cart so that he can travel in style.

The financial planner may not ever be able to untie or cut all the ropes. This may be because the client doesn't believe he will ever get loose and will just keep rolling along in his comfort zone (the rut) at his own pace. It could be that the client is afraid to turn loose from the wheel because it provides security. After all, his father and mother had one just like it and were never untied. He may like the comfort of the circular rut.

The financial consultant must give client a map that will take him to the top of the mountain. Remember that the map prepared for the client may not take him all the way to the top. It will not be a perfect map. The financial planner has a general idea of the direction to the top, but is not sure how well the client can drive his cart or whether he can make repairs or adjustments. However, the planner is relatively sure he can design a map that will take him at least as far as the third or fourth plateau on the mountain. When an airplane leaves Dallas for New York, I am told that it is off course roughly 95 percent of the time. Constant minor course corrections are made to bring it back on course. The corrections are made easily because there is a known course to follow and a known destination. The same is true for a financial road map. Course corrections are made regularly. Remember that financial planning is a process, not an event.

When I first entered financial planning, I had a lot of trouble getting started because I couldn't untie all the ropes at once, much less design a map to reach the top of the mountain. I either didn't know how or the client wouldn't sit still long enough for me to do the work. Often he wouldn't share his goals (the key). It was my opinion that if I couldn't untie all the ropes and take him to the top of the mountain, then I had no business working with the client at all. Then it dawned on me that if I could untie only one of the ropes, I had done the client a service. Although still tied to the wheel and still in the rut, the client might be able to enjoy a little less pressure from one of the nine ropes. Blood circulation might improve after removing one of the constraints. It might even spur him into giving me enough information to untie the rest. Then we could go from there to designing a map to the top of the mountain. Again, our first steps may not be giant leaps to the top but gradual climbing of one plateau at a time. If he just reaches the first plateau, look how far he has come. Though not at the top of the mountain and possibly unlikely to ever get there, isn't he better off than he was in the rut tied to the wheel?

Dealing with the Spokes and the Ropes

Are you starting to understand what a financial planner does? She releases clients from the traditional financial constraints and obstacles with which most of us are bound. Then she designs a road map or maps to take the client to stage 9 of mastery over money—*Freedom, Balance, and Generosity.* All along the journey, the financial planner counsels clients to keep them on their journeys. It sounds simple because it basically is. Most financial planning is common sense. Certainly some technical knowledge, product knowledge, and people skills are required, but these represent icing on the cake. Once you have the cake, adding icing will come naturally.

Remember that there are nine spokes. They weren't listed in order of importance, just random order. For some clients, spoke 9 might be the most important spoke and possibly the only one that you need to deal with at first. For others, it will be spoke 2 or 5.

Risk and Insurance

For many clients, this spoke, risk and insurance, is integrally related to spoke 7, asset protection. For others, handling risk and insurance has less to do with protecting assets already accumulated than with protecting income streams and providing for families in the event of untimely death or disability. The ropes tying clients to this spoke usually are made up of their income streams, education and job skills, current assets, and family sizes. A good financial consultant will gather as much data as possible about clients and assess their most obvious risk areas. If clients are unable or unwilling to give you the data you need to make a complete assessment, then ask to see their tax returns as a minimum. Ask to see all the clients' current insurance policies. Why did the clients buy them? Are the policies performing the purpose intended when they bought them? Did they buy them for the right purpose? Considering the clients' marital situations, number of children, assets, educational levels, marketable job skills, and income levels, what are their biggest risks? Does their current insurance cover that risk? Keep going down the list to the other risks and evaluate each one accordingly.

Sound complicated? It will be difficult only if you choose to make it that way. Most people are managing risks so poorly that the errors will literally jump out at you. They are either under- or overinsured, have the wrong kind of insurance, or are insuring the wrong risks. For example, many clients will be loaded up on life insurance policies on the kids with relatively little or no coverage on the income stream of the primary wage earner. Children have tremendous spiritual value but little economic value. They have no income stream to protect. If they die, it will be a tremendous personal loss but will not compare economically to the loss suffered if a parent dies. Many clients have a great deal of insurance on their lives, but none for disability. Yet they are roughly three times more likely to suffer some type of disability than they are to die prematurely.

Remember to practice holistic financial planning when working on this spoke. Try for balance, not perfection. If you get clients' insurance situations in *perfect* order, you will very likely leave no disposable income to deal with their other problems. Just handle the most glaring problems first.

Investments

Investments are the spoke with which financial consultants feel most comfortable. It is also the area that most of the general public sees as a financial planner's primary value. The ropes tying clients to this spoke are usually made up of risk tolerance, emergency funds, long- and short-term goals, and current investments. Again, the data-gathering process will tell the financial planner most of what he or she needs to know. What are clients trying to accomplish with their investments? What are their short- and long-range goals? Do the investments match those? Do they match clients' risk tolerances? It is not unusual to find a very conservative client invested in high-risk assets. How does this happen? Bad advice. A good salesperson may have played on the client's need for instant gratification and pure greed. Do clients say they want to retire in 10 years but can realistically reach that goal in no less than 20? Ask questions. Record the answers. Evaluate where clients are versus where they want to go.

I often use the *treasure chest approach* when working with clients. I ask the clients to visualize their money in treasure chests. Each chest represents one of their goals. I also ask that they have at least one chest labeled as an emergency fund. Usually chest 2 is called the *big expense fund*. This is where the client regularly deposits money to handle those big expenses that inevitably come along. They may be planned, such as paying for auto insurance or house insurance on an annual basis, or unplanned, such as replacement of a major appliance that breaks. The other necessary chest is for retirement. We tell the client that this one has a lock on it and should not be touched until retirement. Make it something to look forward to rather than a painful experience. The younger the clients, the more likely they are to see it as painful to put money back for such a long period. The remaining chests are for the clients' goals. After clients are tuned into this approach, the rest is fairly easy. Just match the investment's nature to the nature of the trunks. Long-term investments and those carrying the most risk go in the longer-term trunks. Short-term investments such as emergency funds go in the short-term trunks.

Asset allocation has become so popular in the last few years that it is now a buzzword in the industry. Most financial planners understand it, but many clients do not. Don't use the term with clients unless they understand it. Ask a few questions to determine their levels of understanding, then adjust your explanation to clients' levels. The principle behind asset allocation is rather simple. Based on Nobel prize–winning research, the theory is that the more classes of assets we use to make up our portfolio, the less the risk and the higher the rate of return. By asking clients some questions about risk tolerance and goals, investment policy statements can be developed. From these statements, certain percentages of clients' portfolios can be allocated according to predetermined model portfolios that have been developed from extensive research. For clients with high risk tolerance, the model portfolio will have higher percentages invested in aggressive investments such as small cap growth and value stocks. For the very conservative client, model portfolios will lean toward more conservative investments such as blue chip stocks and highly rated corporate and government bonds.

Taxes

If you don't have a background in taxation, the word probably strikes fear in your heart. We all know the extent of the ropes (or nooses) that tie people to this spoke. After having prepared or reviewed more than 9,000 tax returns, trust me when I say that you will never make sense out of the code. It simply makes neither economic nor logical sense. In my other book, *Financial Planning for CPAs*, I have a chapter entitled "Taxes for Non-Tax Pros." In this chapter, I explore the components of the basic tax return. Until Congress takes action to demolish the code, taxes are something that you and your clients must deal with in the financial planning process. Fortunately, getting connected to this profession will lead you to many sources for good training on how to deal with taxes and to advise your clients about them.

Not having experience in tax returns may not be as great a disadvantage as you might think. Many seasoned tax professionals cannot see the forest for the trees. They get so caught up in the intricacies of preparing a tax return that they forget to look at it for more client opportunities. When studying taxes, be sure to learn the difference between deductions and credits (deductions are against income that is subject to tax and credits are against taxes). It doesn't take a genius to see that a credit is more beneficial.

Also learn the difference between gross income and adjusted gross income, how the standard deduction and itemized deductions interact, and the difference between deductions and exemptions. Once you learn these basics, use your own tax returns and those of your clients to learn from experience. Try copying your and your clients' tax returns and marking up the copies to see how various changes in income, deductions, and credits might affect the tax due. Also, you must know how to calculate the value of a tax-deferred investment versus a taxable one and one that is tax free. You can do this using a financial calculator and a little common sense.

Until you become tax wise, keep a cheat sheet handy to check on your clients' tax statuses. Your cheat sheet might contain the following reminders for you and your client:

Is the client getting full benefit from itemized deductions? Most people are barely exceeding the standard deduction and do not realize that their itemized deductions are yielding minor benefits. If they are not yielding much in direct benefit, this could be a signal to pay off a house mortgage, for example.

Is the client paying taxes that are compatible to the peer group? If the client is paying more than average, the return needs examination.

Is the client taking advantage of basic tax planning ideas?

Tax-deferred annuities

Tax-exempt investments

Retirement plans that are tax deferred such as IRAs, SEPs, and 401Ks

Again, experience is the best teacher. Even without being a tax expert, you can quickly learn how to read a tax return and evaluate whether the client is taking care of the basics. Don't forget to ask questions that allow you to determine how important tax avoidance is to the client. Many clients will try to avoid taxes at the expense of good judgment, whereas others don't hate the IRS that much.

Raising and Educating Children

Most financial plans only plan for educational expenses. I like to include weddings, unusual athletic expenses, unusually high social expenses (such as particular fraternities or sororities), special training such as music lessons, expensive hobbies that parents wish to encourage, and so forth. Again, this spoke is as complicated as clients want to make it. The ropes here might be the level of education to which clients and their children aspire, public or private colleges and universities, likelihood of scholarship, age of children when planning is begun, sex of children (the wedding thing), tactic of preparation (going for grants or public assistance or paying your own way), or risk tolerance.

This is probably the easiest of the spokes to manage. Although some cases can be complicated by the possibility of obtaining grants or student loans, most are a function of the age of the children and the level of education desired. Preparing to pay your own way may directly conflict with qualifying for grants. I have found this conflict to be relatively easily resolved in my own practice. I simply choose not to engage in assisting clients in preparing for grants or loans unless they are sure that this is the only route available and they specifically request my assistance in reaching their goals. If the child is more than six years away from college, I advise clients to set aside funds in case the grants and loans are discontinued or unavailable for any reason.

Other choices that the normal client will need assistance with include the choice of investment type and in whose name they should be. This will be too simply stated for my colleagues who love complexity, but my rules are these: The closer the client is to college, the more conservative and liquid the investment must be. The longer the period before college, the more appropriate are investments that offer larger returns commensurate with risk. As for whose name to put the investments in, I usually recommend gifting and putting them in the child's name under the Uniform Gifts to Minors Act or Uniform Transfers to Minors Act. Congress has added "kiddie tax" rules to the code, but they rarely affect my decision to give the money to the kids to save taxes. Be familiar with them and do your calculations. In most cases, the child will still be in the lowest bracket. If a client is transferring big bucks to a kid under 14, some serious tax planning is needed, but that is the exception rather than the rule.

How does one go about finding out the costs of education at a particular college today? There are many sources. Obviously, you can call the college, but this sometimes results in a bureaucratic maze. Product sponsors, your broker-dealer, most of the professional designation sponsors, and many others can provide not only the information you need but also software to project costs year by year and to calculate the amount needed to invest. One hint: always know the costs for the universities close to your area. If you have a child in college or one who has completed, be ready with true stories about your experiences.

As you become more educated about financial planning, you will also read a lot about the dangers of transferring funds to minors in order to plan for their educations, weddings, and so forth. The stories usually involve the child gaining custody of the assets at age 18 or 21 (depending on the state), then squandering them instead of going to college. This makes for a good story, but it follows the usual pattern of a lot of writers in the financial profession. They write more about the exceptional situations than the general ones because they make more interesting stories. I know that this has happened, but in my 20-plus years of dealing with client financial matters, I have never had it happen to a client. You get paid to see that it doesn't happen. Simply don't give the kid enough details to derail your plans for his education. If a parent announces to a teenager "I have $50,000 set aside for your education down at the bank. Here's a copy of the account. At age 18, you can do with it as you please, but please use it for education," then the parent may deserve for the kid to go driving off in a new $40,000 sports car in the opposite direction from college.

Emergency and Goals Funding Cash Flow

This spoke has several ropes binding it. Most clients don't have an emergency fund. I have seen many cases where clients were actively trading individual stocks in margin accounts but did not have an emergency fund. I usually tell clients that such a fund is a necessity before we can work together. If they don't have the funds or the income stream to really put one together fast, then I will put them on a bank draft program into a money market account until they have enough assets to qualify as a minimum emergency fund. Then we can work on other goals. When I can get clients to reveal the goals that they have other than the standard ones of quality retirement and education planning, they usually get excited about the financial planning process. As stated previously, a key element of financial planning is helping clients to reframe their views of saving and investing. Most people view it as punishment, but if you can get them to connect regular investing to a very pleasing vision of their goals, then they will willingly participate in the process and stick to it when times get tough. I view this ability to get clients connected to their own dreams or visions as the best attribute of a quality financial consultant.

Very often, I simply can't get a young couple to plan for retirement. They don't think that I understand about things such as raising kids, mortgage payments, car and appliance repairs, or car payments. They can't see themselves ever retiring; it is just too far in the future. However, they can usually articulate a dream of owning a home and a nice car and traveling. This has often been my ticket to entering them into the financial planning process. I may have to forget retirement talk for the present. Once I get them to start investing toward shorter-term goals, I can easily move them into retirement planning.

The biggest hurdle for most clients, young and old, is cash flow. Very few clients have money left over at the end of the month. If they are just getting by on $100,000 a year, they don't seem to notice that the folks down the block are doing just fine on $60,000 a year. Those earning $60,000 don't notice that people are getting by just fine on $40,000. They all ask the same question: Where does it all go? The answer is that lifestyle expands to absorb any additional income. Unfortunately, life's *quality* doesn't always expand in direct proportion to your income. Most people just start wasting money because it is there to waste. We are still essentially hunters and gatherers. We like to gather as many "things" as possible when times are good. The financial consultant's role here is to get clients to take charge of their lives. It is simply a matter of making a habit of planning where you are going. Once a plan is in place, you can have much more fun and enjoyment out of the money.

How does one get control? Do you tell clients that we are going to do cash flow planning? That we are going to put them on a budget? No! I never mention the B-word to clients. Certainly budgets and controlling expenses are good. However, I don't have one and don't think most clients will sit still to prepare one. Nor will they give you enough data to prepare one. Even if you could gather enough data on spending patterns to prepare a budget, I don't think the client could afford to pay you for the time it would take. Also, who is going to monitor the budget? You? Again, I think that economic reality for both you and the client is going to prevent this. There are a few clients who need and can afford to pay for this, but most can't.

So what do we do? My method of cash flow planning or budgeting is simple.

1. Channel all available investment funds into an emergency fund treasure chest.

2. After the emergency fund is established, channel funds (by bank draft, payroll deduction, or other automatic investment) into each treasure chest. How much do you channel? That is an educated guess. Try to use clients' income streams, their levels of commitment to the goals, their prior

spending habits, their self-discipline, and their knowledge about basic ways to cut back on spending. Again, this is what you get paid to do. Ask questions, gather data, but don't get so caught up in the analysis that you don't make a recommendation. The plan or the amounts are not going to be perfect. Remember what I said about the plane being off course 95 percent of the time?

If clients remain unconvinced that there are leaks in their spending habits, you may need to take a more disciplined look at their finances. However, I have found that most leaks are obvious by a casual look at clients and their lifestyles. Is she driving overpriced cars? Has he overbought on a house? Is he a clotheshorse? Most spending leaks are not gushers. If they are gushers, the clients usually know where they are and you manage them. Common leaks include the following:

Buying things because they are on sale and not because you need them

Shopping without a purpose other than entertainment

Eating out too much

Overbuying clothes

Overbuying car, home, and health insurance and buying the wrong kind

Impulse buying

Carrying credit card balances

Carrying too much cash

Not knowing how to buy the basic necessities

I found that you can lecture your clients until you lose your voice on these matters, but until they start having their excess funds channeled into the treasure chests, they won't change their habits. If you can get them to stay with the program for six months, they are hooked. If they stay a year, they are lifers. They will proactively seek out ways to save money on purchases so that they can have more money for the things that really contribute to a better life.

Still don't believe me? Look around at TV infomercials. People are starved for the basics of how to live better financial lives. They pay so-called financial gurus hundreds of dollars for books and memberships in order to find out basic things like when to raise the deductible on their car or home insurance and when to drop everything except liability. Meanwhile, the sophisticated financial planners are selling portfolio optimization, standard deviations, risk-adjusted returns, and so forth. There is certainly a place for this type of information, but be sure that what you are providing matches what clients want and need.

Retirement Planning

The ropes tying clients to this spoke also come in various shapes and sizes. Planning for retirement for anyone younger than age 45 was very difficult for me at first. The likelihood of being wrong about projections going to 20 years or more is great. That scared me. Again, I was more concerned about the correctness of my projections than I was about helping clients. Very often, financial consultants will prepare plans more for other financial planning professionals or academia than for their clients. We always want to prepare plans that we would be proud to show our colleagues. We want them to be examples of politically correct planning. There is nothing wrong with that ambition, unless it gets in the way of serving your clients' needs.

Like the other spokes in the wheel, we can make untying or cutting the ropes that bind clients as complicated as we want. Who knows what inflation will be for the next 20 or 30 years? Anybody want to guess about tax rates? The stock or bond market? Interest rates? This is a clear prescription for paralysis by analysis. My advice is to not get too hung up in looking at the trees before you look at the forest. In fact, I look at this long time span as simplifying the process rather than complicating it. I have found that planning for a retirement that is to take place in five years or less requires a great deal more time than planning for one that takes place 20 years from now. There is much less room for error in the shorter retirement. Remember my analogy about the plane that stays off course 95 percent of the time but still reaches its destination. The bulk of my retirement planning is done on one sheet for each client. It is called the financial security planning worksheet and calculates *the gap*. My components of financial planning for retirement are as follows:

1. Determine today's living expenses. This figure can be a real brain teaser because it is not available on some form somewhere and the clients usually don't have a clue as to what they are spending. If data are scarce and time is short, I will usually just use a percentage of today's gross income from the tax return. If clients don't have a good feel as to specifics about lifestyle in retirement, I will usually use around 80 percent. I don't get hung up on before and after taxes or year-by-year withdrawals unless the retirement is imminent and more exact numbers are required.

2. Estimate living expenses at retirement in future dollars. This is just a function of the number of years until retirement and an inflation rate applied to number 1. I let clients estimate inflation. If they don't have a clue, I use the historical average of about 4 percent.

3. Subtract known benefits that clients will have provided from other sources such as retirement plans at work, Social Security, or trusts. In the beginning, I had more problems with this number than any other. Then I realized that for longer-term forecasts, we were not going to be accurate no matter how hard we analyzed. If the information about company retirement plans was readily available and accurate, I used it. If not, I used a standard percentage for corporate retirement plans of 30 percent of number 2. I usually don't include Social Security benefits for clients younger than age 35. For those older than that, I use today's maximum benefit because I have little faith in Social Security.

4. Net annual income required from investments. This is number 3 subtracted from number 2.

5. Value of investments needed for retirement. This is number 4 divided by an expected after-tax rate of return. I usually use a rate of a couple of percentage points below the going return for a relatively conservative investment portfolio.

6. Net earning assets needed. This is number 5 less the value of any assets that will be liquidated at retirement to turn into earning assets. This can be real estate, businesses, equipment, hobby collections, and so forth.

You now have a number to work with. It may not be accurate, but it is a start. Now you can look at what clients have versus what they need and calculate the gap. The next step is to compute how much your clients will need to invest monthly to fill this gap (a simple financial calculator function).

I realize that there are all sorts of nuances working here. For example, I didn't consider the spend down of principal. I don't do before- and after-tax calculations on all the living expense numbers. I think using gross expenses is just as accurate. Whether you are paying taxes or spending the money elsewhere, you still need it. However, I can use these variations to my advantage rather than having them tie me and my clients up with meaningless analysis. For example, if the gap is simply too large to fill in the time frame that clients have before retirement, I may recalculate a spend down of principal. I don't like to do this, because I don't know when clients are going to die. Sometimes it is necessary, however. I also will often do two phases to retirement: the early healthy years followed by the later, less-healthy years. I often save certain assets for those later years in a detailed analysis. I never, however, let these later manipulations take my sights off the original goal—the accumulation of a certain amount of money to accommodate a good lifestyle in retirement.

What happens if the amount I calculate as the gap is too large to fill even when I assume the liquidation of principal? Then I really start to earn my money with this client. Depending on the clients' levels of sophistication and willingness to work with me, I will usually discuss the problem and get them to recognize that either they have to make more money or scale back their expectations. I need to prepare them for reality. If they are less sophisticated, I often will rework my assumptions to reach a more reasonable goal. I don't want clients to get the idea that they are in an impossible situation or they may adopt a hopeless attitude and freeze. My more academic colleagues can easily find fault and say that I am playing with the numbers. I am. That is what I was doing when I made the original calculations, also. That is what we all do. Prove my assumptions wrong, if you can. Our ultimate purpose is to start clients on the journey to a good retirement. As long as clients are fully informed about what assumptions have been made in order to reach the target, they may keep their thoughts and vision focused where we want them to be.

The second major step in retirement planning is the choice of methods to fund retirement. Taxes play a major role here. I usually ask my clients to visualize this treasure chest as having a large lock on it. They hold the key to that lock. Unless they decide to open it and take out some money, the IRS is kept at bay. Almost all retirement plans are tax deferred. Look at the options available to clients and make sure they take maximal advantage of them. If they are maxed out at work or in their own businesses, they may qualify for other types of tax-deferred investments such as non-qualified retirement plans or tax-deferred annuities. When I am discussing how much clients should put into a retirement plan, my first goal is to always go as high as the law allows. Many people simply can't afford this, but most can afford more than they think. If payroll deduction is available, it is a great way to get into the habit of saving.

The final step is to choose the type of investments. This is usually easy. If there is a company plan, it will usually have six or more choices. Allocating among the six is usually the same as in any asset allocation program. People often forget to look at the rest of clients' portfolios when allocating assets in a retirement plan, however. The first inclination is to fund most of the retirement with long-term equity investments because of the long-term nature of any retirement fund. However, if clients already have a lot of equities outside their retirement plans I may lean toward income-producing assets such as high-yield bonds. My reasoning is that these bonds outside of a retirement plan often throw off lots of taxable income. Inside the plan, that income is tax deferred.

Like most of the other spokes, retirement planning means keeping your eyes on the goal and helping your clients to visualize the goal. Part of retirement planning may extend to the emotional aspects of leaving jobs and careers. Clients' identities may be wholly or partially tied to their careers. Talk about these issues along with the financial ones. Invite a professional psychologist to speak about retirement at one of your seminars.

Asset Protection

There are ways to describe the relationship between people and their money other than the stages of mastery over money. The first phase could be stated as earning and spending, the second as accumulation, the third as accumulation and protection, and the fourth as spending and protection. Protection of assets in this context is different than protection under ordinary insurance. As clients accumulate assets today, they become increasingly vulnerable to attacks on those assets. We have become a litigious society. Our civil justice system encourages a system of "going for the deepest pockets." Clients can be involved in minor auto accidents and lose their entire life savings in court. A car can be stolen and the owner held responsible for damage that the thief does to others while driving the car. If a client is self-employed, the chances for being sued multiply. Employees can get hurt on the job and break a company. There are literally dozens of methods used to attack the financially secure.

The financial consultant's role in asset protection is to advise clients about the dangers that exist and find ways to afford as much protection for their assets as possible. Some of the methods to be used include the following:

1. Review all insurance coverage to be sure it is adequate. Consider umbrella insurance for exposed areas or under-coverage in specific areas. Umbrella insurance is relatively inexpensive and can be added to other insurance protection at predetermined limits.
2. Review documents before clients sign. Be sure they don't obligate themselves for contingent liabilities larger than their fair share.
3. Use the proper form of business organization that affords the most protection.
4. Choose investments that are protected from suit. In some states IRAs and deferred annuities are protected.
5. For more sophisticated or risky situations, consult an attorney to set up trusts and family limited partnerships.

Old Age and Elder Care Planning

In chapter 1, I gave you some statistics about the graying of America. Older adults represent one of the most exciting and innovative areas in financial planning today. The fastest growing age group in America is the over 85 set. There are more than 52,000 centenarians (people older than 100) in America today. That represents three times the number living in 1980. The message for the young is to start saving more because they will be retired about as many years as they work. Or maybe the message is that they will work longer. We will find that out as time passes. We must start rethinking our concepts about old age; it is no longer 65.

People preparing for retirement today cannot just plan on living about 15 years after retirement. They are living more than twice that long. Financial planners must train clients of all age levels about these changes. For example, some say that a baby born in the year 2000 can expect to live to age 140 if these trends continue. This creates opportunities such as the following:

1. Assisting clients with planning for two, three, or more careers
2. Planning for possible long-term health care
   a. Evaluating nursing homes and assisted-living facilities
   b. Long-term health care insurance
   c. Learning how to qualify for Medicaid if that remains an option
3. Reevaluation of personal residence values and taking another look at townhomes or condominiums
4. Planning for incapacity with living wills, durable powers of attorney, and living trusts
5. Changing thoughts about investments for older adults; equities and growth assets are now expected to stay in the picture longer

Transfer Planning

This spoke of the wheel probably has more types of ropes tying clients than any other. It is also the one they are most likely to ignore and probably the last one they will let you untie or cut. It may even have a lock. The key to this lock must be provided by clients as they tell you what they want to happen upon their deaths. One of Uncle Sam's most onerous taxes is the estate tax. Just in case clients are able to save in spite of tax and other laws that discourage it, just in case they exercise good judgment and build up retirement funds so that they will not be a burden to society, the government is ready with a new set of taxes at graveside.

Most states also have onerous and unfair state laws in place to take away your assets if you do not plan around these laws.

Enter the financial consultant. Your role is to reduce these complicated rules to simple terms in order to communicate the need for planning to your clients. Estate planning is an area with which I had a lot of trouble because the laws are so complex. I hated doing estate tax returns because the instructions were written in more confusing language than the rest of the tax code. Also, the person who owned the estate was not around to answer questions. After attending literally dozens of seminars and workshops on estate planning, I discovered that I did not have to be an expert in estate planning to assist my clients. I just had to be able to identify problems in my clients' personal situations and point them out. I could also propose general solutions, but more complicated situations could be worked out by a person with estate-planning expertise, usually an attorney who has experience in complicated estate matters.

Estate planning can be reduced to its simplest form before delving into the complexities of solving individual clients' situations.

1. How do clients feel about the transfer of their assets upon death? Many don't think they care. Many care a lot and want to retain control after death. Most want to do everything possible to protect their loved ones.

2. Instructions for the transfer of assets and the use of assets while clients are alive but incapacitated must be put in writing *in advance.* This means wills and trusts. Otherwise, the state will make decisions about clients' assets that may adversely affect clients or their heirs. Also, the wrong people may wind up with the wrong assets. Loved ones may be treated unfairly or left out altogether unless clients state their wishes in writing in advance.

3. Wills and trusts must be written in such a way that transfer taxes are kept to a minimum. Otherwise, more than 50 percent of the assets could wind up in the hands of the government. Another 25 percent or more could go to lawyers. Taxes can be reduced by several methods:
   Giving assets away before death

Giving up control of assets before death through trusts but retaining income

Giving assets to charity before or after death while retaining income

Writing wills and trusts to take maximal advantage of the marital deduction and the unified credit

4. After all measures have been taken to reduce taxes, the estate must be analyzed for liquidity. If there are not enough liquid assets in the estate to pay the estate taxes that remain after careful planning, the problem must be solved using insurance or other methods. Otherwise, nonliquid assets in the estate may have to be sold at bargain prices to generate enough money to pay the taxes. In almost all cases, the taxes are due nine months after death.

The financial consultant's role in the transfer process is critical. It can involve working with attorneys and other estate-planning experts, the client, and the client's partners, employees, business associates, and heirs. The planner is usually in the role of a team captain in a transfer-planning situation and must determine the client's wishes and ensure that they are carried out for the least fees, taxes, and time.

CLIMBING THE MOUNTAIN

Which comes first, the chicken or the egg? The ropes and spokes or the map? I'm afraid the answer is not going to be clear. Both must be worked on at the same time. Generally speaking, working on the ropes and spokes will produce the map. However, there are instances when you can easily solve existing problems while you are working on the map. Clients may not want maps at this time. They may not even be able to think about the mountain until you get them out of the rut or at least partially untied. The map referred to is, of course, the financial plan. A further complicating issue is that a lot of my maps are constructed in pieces over time. I may construct maps for each spoke or for several spokes at once but not for all spokes. It depends on the clients and their situations.

How do you construct a financial plan? The most basic of steps in the financial planning process are as follows:

1. Gather data from the client
2. Prepare the financial plan
3. Achieve harmony with the client on the value of the plan
4. Implement the plan
5. Monitor the plan

Gathering Data

I don't like to gather data. Some people are good at it. I am not. I designed modular packages to make the process easier. Also, the forms are designed so that staff members can ask the questions and obtain the data before you get involved. You should gather your own data until you are experienced in the process, however. I use seven modular packages for gathering data.

1. Personal and family data
2. Goals and investment philosophy
3. Financial data
4. Income and expenses
5. Insurance policy listing
6. Estate planning data
7. Advisor and document listing

Packages 1 and 2 are essential to any plan, no matter how condensed; package 3 is essential to most plans.

Preparing the Financial Plan

These are the parts of my financial plans:

1. Introduction
2. Goals
3. Plan summary

4. Assets available to reach goals

5. Assets required to reach goals

6. The gap

7. Insurance planning

8. Health, elder care, and incapacity planning

9. Transfer planning

10. Recommendations

11. Asset allocation

12. Prospectuses, applications, brochures, contracts, agreements

13. Implementation instructions

Sounds time-consuming and complicated, doesn't it? I remind you that I seldom use more than six parts. Although a complete description of how to build a financial plan is beyond the scope of this work, I will briefly describe the use of each part.

The *introduction* consists of a simple but appropriate cover sheet with the client's name and a brief title of the type of plan. I occasionally add a cover letter. It also should include a table of contents.

Goals include a description of the objectives clients have provided to you. They are the key component of the plan. They can be as simple or as complex as the clients allow. When I am preparing a plan, I print the goals immediately and put them in plain sight so that I can repeatedly refer to them in my creative process. I have prepared plans with only one goal and plans with as many as 25 goals. Most plans include about six major goals, which can sometimes be as simple as "to invest $100,000 to earn the maximum possible return consistent with my moderately conservative risk profile with some tax advantage." If clients cannot identify a goal, you cannot prepare a plan. You must ask enough questions to get clients to open up to you and confide what they want to achieve. If clients have persistent problems identifying their goals, I provide them with a list of common goals and ask them to first check the ones that are important to them, then rate their importance on a scale of 1 to 10. I always leave space at the bottom for writing in goals. This spurs the thought process. Clients are invariably receptive to this process, because they like thinking about their fondest hopes.

Plan summary is usually included only in larger plans. I use this section to summarize the goals in more general terms and to give a brief description of what we are trying to accomplish with the plan. It is similar to the recommendations section but not as specific.

Assets available to meet goals is just a statement of financial condition—a balance sheet for the client. I consider this the second most important part of the plan. Most clients react enthusiastically to seeing their own balance sheets. I don't use accounting jargon on mine. For example, assets are called *What I Own* and liabilities are called *What I Owe*. When discussing with clients, I call it the *Where You Are Today* statement. Most clients have never had their personal net worth calculated. I refer to this amount as their *Get Out of Town Amount*—or how big would the check have to be to buy you out? It always makes people think. In many, it causes a complete change in their perspective of financial matters forever. They start making financial decisions based on whether it will increase or decrease their net worth.

Assets required to meet goals may take two different approaches. Using other pieces of the plan, I may construct a *Balance Sheet of the Future* or a statement of *Where You Want to Be*. In most cases, however, it is a goal-by-goal statement showing how much it will take to accomplish each goal. For example, if one of the goals is to educate a child, I quantify the costs and project those costs into the years when the child will reach college age.

The gap, as discussed earlier in the retirement spoke, is simply the difference that must be accumulated in order to reach the clients' goals. It may involve the difference between funds available and funds required to purchase a new home, for example. It may also involve a simple calculation of the future value of a $100,000 investment at various rates of return to illustrate the risk-reward principle.

Insurance planning is usually a listing of various policies. I may offer a comparison of the value of assets insured versus insurance held or a calculation of the amount of life and disability insurance held versus the amount that should be held. I may also compare types of insurance held with my recommendations.

Health, elder care, and incapacity planning is usually in plans for clients older than 40. Occasionally, when doing complete plans for younger clients, I will also include this section, recommending certain steps for the clients' parents. This section will usually discuss the problems clients have in this area or general discussion about the need for planning.

Transfer planning includes a projected estate size at death. I will usually use normal life expectancy for men and women to estimate time of death. I then estimate the amount of transfer taxes due. I normally do a liquidity analysis after the taxes are estimated. Although this sounds complicated, it is an estimate only and very easy to prepare. I usually use the *assets available* section to calculate the approximate estate size. Tax calculations are from tables. Software is available, but I seldom use it at this stage. To determine liquidity problems, I simply subtract liquid assets from the estate taxes. If there is a deficiency, I will discuss with the client what may happen to nonliquid assets.

Recommendations are just that. I usually reduce them to bullet points and put them in sequential order or order of importance (without excess verbiage).

Asset allocation models are occasionally included in my plans, but not very often. If the primary focus of the plan is investments, I might include a comparison of where the assets are currently invested to my recommended allocation. I often use simple pie charts side by side to illustrate the difference.

Prospectuses, applications, and brochures are seldom included in my financial plans because they are too bulky. I seldom mention products in my plans, so prospectuses are not required at this stage. I will have them ready for client review when we are ready to discuss and implement the plan.

Implementation instructions are provided for internal staff or as reminders for me as to the actual procedural steps to implement the plan. For example, the implementation instructions might include which of the client's holdings to sell and where to reinvest the proceeds.

Achieving Harmony with the Client on the Plan

I suppose this stage could be called the sales process. Just because you prepared nice financial plans doesn't mean that clients are going to implement them. If they don't, you have done a lot of work that has little value. You may get paid anyway, but you probably won't get many referrals. If implementation is the way you get paid, then you certainly won't receive compensation if a client doesn't take action. That is why I believe you must go through the thought-provoking and creative process that is required to create a good financial plan. If you have been through that process, you will believe in the plan enough to transfer that belief to the client.

I recommend that you or your assistant call the client and set up an appointment after the plan is prepared, but before it is mailed or delivered to the client. Unless you have charged the client in advance for the plan, it belongs to you until the client pays for or implements it. You at least have the right to an appointment before turning it over. After the appointment is set, I recommend mailing or delivering the plan to the client at least five days before the scheduled appointment. This gives the client plenty of time to review it before and come fully prepared to discuss it at your appointment. If clients do not review the plan before the meeting, it is their fault and not yours. I believe that the client should implement part or all of the plan at the first meeting. A lot of financial planners believe that the process takes as many as six or more meetings over several months. That sounds good, but people make decisions based on emotions, and most will be emotionally drained after more than a couple of meetings. If you are charging by the hour, they are also going to become a little fee-sensitive. Many clients are simply let's-do-it people. There is a matter of economics for the financial planner, also. If clients' assets are not all that large, there is an economic maximum that they can afford to pay and that the financial planner can afford to spend in time. I will discuss other sales tactics in chapter 7.

Implementing the Plan

Implementing the plan simply involves doing the steps in the recommendations. Completion may take several months or even years. As mentioned previously, I like to at least reach agreement in principle at the first meeting after the plan is prepared. The implementation instructions become more valuable as time goes by and memory fades. If you want to receive maximal value for your time, you will enter all steps that were not implemented into a time-management system for follow-up with the client at a later date. This is a much more productive use of your time than soliciting new clients, because the client has a plan that is already prepared and partially implemented.

Monitoring the Plan

Monitoring the plan is an ongoing process. The financial consultant takes the client through several steps of implementation and records the results of each phase as it is accomplished. If recommended steps remain incomplete, the planner must follow up with the client to ensure that all steps are completed. I also include in this step the periodic reporting of the investments' performances. This is important and valuable to both the client and the financial planner. If clients see progress being made toward their goals, they will implement any remaining steps, invest more money, and give you referrals.

These are the steps in the financial planning process and the creation of a financial plan. Use them in your practice. A lot of people calling themselves planners do not actually prepare many financial plans. Plans require creative effort and a lot of start-up time. However, they are invaluable in becoming a successful financial consultant of the future. See Appendix C for a sample financial plan.

I hope that the wheel and spoke and mountain map analogies helped to illustrate the financial planning process. I operate in a pragmatic world, not a perfect one. None of my financial planning engagements have ever fit perfectly into the pages of a textbook on financial planning. Many came close, but more were far removed. However, that does not mean that the client was not helped. Keep the process moving and you can reach the top of the mountain yourself.

3

WHO IS PROVIDING FINANCIAL PLANNING TODAY?

The fact that 30,000 people held the certified financial planner (CFP) designation in 1995 (50 percent more than in 1990) could be positive or negative for those wishing to enter the profession. It could mean that the profession is overcrowded, that the train has already left the station. One major brokerage firm in this country has almost 12,000 financial consultants. Should an aspiring financial planner then look elsewhere for a career because this one is already overcrowded? I think not. I don't know the actual number of people who call themselves financial planners, consultants, or investment executives. The wave sweeping over the profession and the industry is of such proportions that it really may not matter how many consultants there are now. Most do not practice financial planning the way it will be practiced in the year 2000 and beyond.

The image of the profession has undergone highs and lows and is currently moving up. However, Barbara L. N. Roper, director of investor protection for the Consumer Federation of America, says that the current system makes it easy for con artists to thrive in financial planning. The problems Roper discusses include the conflict of interest issue between fee-only and commission planners, the alphabet soup of professional designations, a lax regulatory environment, and vague definitions of what a planner does. Of course, what else would she say in her position? I believe that consumers are confused about financial planning; however, I remain unconvinced that a stricter regulatory environment will weed out the "bad guys."

Trying to legislate integrity and competence has consistently failed. The accounting profession, for example, has the Certified Public Accountant (CPA) designation as its pinnacle and standard of excellence. However, that standard does not keep many incompetent and unethical CPAs from practicing. The public still has to be cautious. Although continuing professional education is required of CPAs, CFPs, and most other professional groups, it does not stop the unethical and incompetent from sitting in on classes and not listening. There are many ways to obtain continuing professional education without learning anything. Having the CPA designation as the standard has not stopped the proliferation of other accounting groups who think of themselves as just as professional, competent, and ethical as CPAs. In fact, these groups are growing. CPAs have only been able to maintain their firm hold on one service—performing certified audits. That would probably be under more pressure if anyone else wanted to do them.

I am drawing parallels between financial planning and accounting because I see some of the same problems in both. The accounting profession has had 50 years to sort out who is really an accountant and who is not and who the public should be wary of. They still have not mastered it. They have succeeded, however, in making the CPA designation well-known to the American public. Now, CPAs are engaged in a massive campaign to change the image they have spent decades cultivating. My point here is that regulations and laws can never be passed to make any profession as pure as the driven snow. I believe that "cream will rise to the top" in this profession, as in any other. However, financial consulting will never be perfect. Trying to make it so is an exercise in futility. The CFP profession has recently started requiring all CFPs to attend a certain number of hours in ethics training. The sessions I have seen thus far are insulting to the intelligence and integrity of anyone attending. I learned about right and wrong a long time ago; my parents taught me not to lie, cheat, or steal. If people have managed to meet the requirements for a CFP professional designation and not learned these things before now, they certainly are not going to learn them in an ethics course.

Those considering entering financial planning must be prepared to find the landscape littered with people who are practicing at various levels of competence and integrity. Be prepared for the holier-than-thou groups who want to rid the profession of all those who do not practice in their chosen styles. Isn't that similar with all other professions and in the world in general? I'm not an advocate of the buyer-beware philosophy in choosing a financial planner; I believe in harsh and swift punishment including banishment from the profession for those who lie, cheat, and steal under the guise of financial consulting. These unethical planners make it difficult for the true professionals. However, I also believe in self-reliance and accepting responsibility for your own actions. There has to be some sort of balance between regulations, enforcement, and responsibility. If we enforced the laws and regulations already on the books rather than concentrating on passing more, the profession would be improved. Of course, that presupposes that we have a civil and criminal justice system that works and that the legal profession is self-regulatory.

As previously indicated, I think the major trend in financial planning today is the transition from a transaction-based business to a relationship-based business. If I were asked for advice on how to choose a financial consultant by consumers today, I would tell them to seek out planners with whom they feel comfortable in having long-term business and personal relationships. If clients don't feel comfortable with individual consultants, they shouldn't use them. I would also mention the credentials, but they do not guarantee competence and integrity.

Who is practicing financial planning today? It is difficult to categorize or label all the professionals out there, because roles often overlap. In the interest of clarity, I will describe three major groups.

1. People who primarily manage money
2. People who primarily recommend people who manage money
3. People who primarily recommend and sell products

Please note my use of the word *primary*. Each group is prone to delve into the activities of the other two. Most aspiring financial planners will be in group 2 or 3 but should be familiar with group 1, because consultants of all groups work together.

PEOPLE WHO PRIMARILY MANAGE MONEY (GROUP 1)

Included in the money-managing group are (1) mutual funds, (2) brokerage houses, (3) insurance companies, (4) banks, and (5) independent money managers. These people go directly to the financial markets and buy and sell financial assets on behalf of their clients.

Mutual funds are investment companies that invest for participants who share common financial goals. They pool their customers' money to buy stocks, bonds, or other assets on behalf of the group as a whole. They are paid a management fee. Some mutual funds pay commissions to the salespeople who sell their funds. Some funds do not pay commissions to salespeople but distribute their funds through other distribution sources such as the print media, the mail, and fee-based financial planners. The people who sell mutual funds may be stockbrokers (registered representatives), financial planners, insurance agents, or any members of group 2 or 3. Even some members of group 1 buy and sell mutual fund shares.

Brokerage houses may directly manage money or evaluate other money managers for their clients using their own consultants. The larger broker-dealers also put together various products including their own mutual funds to be distributed through their sales force—called registered representatives. Larger broker-dealers who own seats on the major stock exchanges are called *wirehouses*. Their registered representatives are a paid sales force whose compensation is directly linked to the amount of sales of products or services. They are provided with office space, research assistance, and are treated as employees.

The registered representatives of an independent broker-dealer are independent contractors. They are registered through their broker-dealer, but the broker-dealer does not usually treat them as employees or provide such things as office space. Independents do not own seats on the major exchanges, so their transactions for individual stocks and bonds must be handled through a clearing firm that does hold a seat on the major exchanges.

Both major brokerage houses and independent firms may have their own in-house money managers and *wrap accounts.* Wrap accounts are managed accounts in which fees for management, transaction costs, and commissions are all handled through a single account for the customer whose funds are being managed. In-house money managers may primarily manage funds by allocating assets among other chosen money managers. The various layers seem confusing but will become clearer as we learn how people get paid. Also, you will learn that your ability to serve your clients is not hampered by as many complications about managing money as it may seem at this point.

Insurance companies' primary investment vehicles are real estate and long-term bonds. Investors can indirectly share in these investments by purchasing annuities and guaranteed investment contracts. When investors buy fixed annuities or guaranteed investment contracts, they are effectively "lending" the insurance company money. The insurance company takes investors' money, reinvests it for larger returns, and keeps the difference. To confuse matters further, insurance companies also offer variable annuities. With a variable annuity, investors choose from the various products available and participate directly in the performance of the investments chosen. Another overlap is that the insurance company usually teams with a mutual fund (investment company) to manage the variable portion of the annuity. These products are usually sold through registered representatives who also hold insurance licenses.

Bank trust departments are the investment management arms of a bank. They take investors' money and invest it directly in financial or other assets, usually for a fee. Sometimes the money is pooled with other investors' money to purchase certain financial assets; other times investors or their trusts own the asset selected by the bank directly.

Independent money managers, also called *investment advisors* or *investment counselors,* manage portfolios of stocks, bonds, and cash. Normally they are paid a fee and do not sell products to the general public except when they are engaged in transactions on behalf of their clients. Truly independent money managers have no affiliation with any brokerage house, insurance company, or bank. They depend on outside consultants for recommendation of their money management services. Independent money managers are registered with the Securities and Exchange Commission as Registered Investment Advisors.

Don't let confusion about the first group called money managers deter you. It will be cleared up later, and most financial planners do not fit into any of the categories in group 1. However, consultants must know how to work with these money managers.

PEOPLE WHO PRIMARILY RECOMMEND PEOPLE WHO MANAGE MONEY (GROUP 2)

I call the second group the advisors, recommenders, planners, and consultants. They are the people who recommend the money managers previously described. There are at least 20,000 money managers to select from and more products than that for planners to choose from. The consultants have several methods of making their recommendations to clients.

If planners are relationship advisers and accounts are large enough to justify the time, they will define the clients' realistic goals and expectations, write investment policy statements with the clients, establish asset allocation strategies, and evaluate the various investment strategies available. Consultants will evaluate money managers, negotiate fees and commissions when applicable, and facilitate communication between the money managers and their clients. They will manage the clients' expectations and periodically report on progress toward their financial goals.

If clients' problems are simple, portfolios are small, or clients simply will not sit still for all the work that should be done, planners must find alternate ways of serving the clients that are not so time intensive. Group 2 planners may move into group 3 sales in order to make their time more profitable. More will be said about that in chapters on how financial planners get paid (chapter 8), what they do (chapter 2), and the real value they bring to their clients (chapter 4). I mention it now to emphasize that there are alternate ways of getting paid and different levels of service (which are entirely ethical and suitable for most clients) that may or may not involve the entire financial planning process.

The planners in the second group may buy and sell stocks, bonds, mutual funds, and other investment products for their clients. They may also recommend their firms' internal money managers or outside money managers. Consultants may charge commissions, asset-based fees, time-based fees, or all three.

Many planners in this group work as registered investment advisors and/or registered representatives of broker-dealers. Today, most work with the independent group of broker-dealers, but many of the large wirehouses are adding group 2 planners or converting group 3 salespersons to this type of planning. I consider myself a planner in group 2, although most of my revenue comes from sales of investment products. Selling investment products is only a method for making the process practical for both the client and the planner.

PEOPLE WHO PRIMARILY RECOMMEND AND SELL INVESTMENT PRODUCTS (GROUP 3)

The third group is primarily transaction oriented. We will call its members stockbrokers and insurance agents for purposes of illustration. Again, most of the members of group 2 also recommend and sell investment products. Group 3 people add value for their clients by selecting investment products that they feel will perform best. They deal primarily in individual securities but will also often sell shares of mutual funds, as well as variable annuities. I include insurance agents in this group, although many belong in group 2. Most agents, however, primarily sell products. They may sell mutual funds along with their life, health, and disability insurance and were among the first to use the term *financial planning*. As a result, a large segment of the public still thinks that those identifying themselves as financial planners are really insurance agents in disguise.

Some of the best financial planners in group 2 began as insurance agents.

To contrast group 3 with people in group 2, visualize yourself in a clothing store in the men's suit section. Let the suits represent investment products. Group 2 planners are walking around with a client looking to see which suit (a) fits the client, (b) the client can afford, (c) is the right fabric, weight, and style, and (d) is suitable to the client's individual tastes.

By contrast, the folks in group 3 have already walked into the suit store and selected a couple or more styles they would like to sell. They bought them in quantity and are standing outside the store looking for clients to fit the suits they have. See the difference?

Now, if everyone in this little scene is competent and has integrity, there is nothing wrong with either approach. The problem comes when group 2 planners don't really go beyond measuring their clients for size and let them walk out with suits that may fit but are the wrong color, material, or quality. A similar problem arises when the group 3 salespeople can't find customers for their limited selection of suits and start marketing the suits as one size fits all. Both events may result in the customers leaving with the wrong suits. Even worse, customers could have been shopping for sweaters and not suits. A case of buyer beware of products? No, it is an example of buyer beware of financial planners. Clients may not be experts on suits and can easily be led astray but need to be pretty good at choosing people to trust. Is it the clients' fault? No. Am I condemning the salespeople in group 3? No. I will explain the reasoning later.

There is nothing inherently wrong with finding a good product and selling a lot of it. The advantage of this approach is that the people who sell only a few products know each product thoroughly. If they can effectively apply that knowledge to real client situations, everyone wins. However, the danger arises when brokers are greedy or desperate to sell the product or if they truly believe that their products are the cure for everything. Doctors should not prescribe surgery or medicine without examinations and neither should financial advisors.

Specialization is a necessity for most of the members of the third group. For example, insurance products are so complicated that advisors can master the intricacies of only a few. The complexity of insurance products and illustrations can have only two explanations. One is that lawyers write the contracts in accordance with arcane and onerous laws and regulations. The other reason is that contracts are written and illustrated in such obtuse fashion to confuse and mislead the consumer, perhaps because most of the products are so heavily loaded with up-front transaction costs. If customers fully understood how their money effectively disappears without return for several years, they might have a problem with investing in insurance policies. I am not condemning the industry for having distribution costs, only for hiding them and placing most of the burden at the front of the contract. Lower loads (distribution costs) and spreading out the distribution costs over a longer period will be the wave of the future.

Specialization is also necessary for stockbrokers, another subgroup of group 3. There are a limited number of stocks and bonds that can be researched adequately, even with today's technology. Some believe that single brokers can effectively follow fewer than ten stocks. *Effectively* is the key word. Brokers may have research at their fingertips on thousands of stocks but can they read and interpret the information on even hundreds of companies? Can they make the phone calls and personal visits to all the companies? Can brokers become familiar with the workings of particular industries, so that they can compare their stock selection to others available in the same industry? Can they meet and evaluate the management of the companies and assess changes in money management? The increased accessibility of information is helpful, but financial consultants must learn to use it to benefit their clients.

Some brokers say that they don't need to personally attend to all these things to effectively pick investments for their clients because they have the huge resources of their brokerage firms to do the research. There is truth to that. However, when brokers totally rely on others to do their research, then they are truly sellers of investment products, not financial planners. That label is certainly acceptable for many traditional stockbrokers. They may never have claimed to be financial planners. They are brokers in the truest sense of the word. Although I believe that transaction-based brokers are shrinking in number as we head toward more relationship-based financial planning, I also believe that there will always be a place for this type of broker.

Stockbrokers often consider themselves to be market timers. They need to be able to tell clients when it is time to be in or out of the market, when to load up on equities versus bonds, and so forth. Prevailing evidence says that market timing doesn't add value for clients. However, most of the research is based on large numbers suggesting that for the industry as a whole, trying to time adds little or no value. In fact, attempts at timing by individual investors usually prove hazardous to their financial health. However, this overwhelming evidence overlooks one thing—human nature. Many people want their financial advisors to tell them when to be in or out of the market. They see that as the financial consultants' primary value.

During a really low period for the profession, this group and some of the first two groups also sold many limited partnerships that had more tax incentive than economic incentive. It is obvious today that many of these limited partnership products were 100 percent tax driven in their structure, with little thought given to economic reality. Many products offered two-to-one or even higher write-offs. When a client invests $100,000 and gets to deduct $200,000 and is in a 50 percent bracket, it is easy to do the math and see that he has no risk. Whether he gets a huge return is almost irrelevant. He will get his money back from Uncle Sam when he files his tax return. This is a perfect instance of something that sounds too good to be true. Many tax deductions were disallowed, and back taxes, penalties, and interest applied. Clients usually had no way to sell their investments. When they were sold, they often got back 10 percent or less of their money. Many still hold these investments and simply can't sell them.

There were other problems even when tax deductions were not disallowed. Many programs required a minimum investment up front with annual investments for several subsequent years in order to keep the program going. Many limited partners also found that their liabilities were not truly limited. During the process of becoming partners, they signed documents that obligated them for portions of huge liabilities beyond their original investments. They took on their share of these liabilities to get even higher tax deductions. In other cases, investors found themselves hit with "phantom income." This was income that was taxable to them through their limited partnership interest but which they did not receive. These limited partnerships did long-term damage to the profession. The industry's largest trade group, the International Association for Financial Planning, shrunk by more than half during this low period. The lesson for aspiring and current financial planners is

> If it sounds too good to be true, it probably is. If you can't understand the basic workings of the product in less than an hour of research, it is probably too complicated for your client to own and for you to sell.

Group 3 members get paid on the number and size of transactions they make on behalf of their clients. Consequently, many feel that there is an inherent conflict of interest between clients and their advisers. I don't disagree. However, it is only fair to state that there are conflicts of interest in group 1 and group 2. In fact, they exist in almost any situation in which either a product or service is being sold. The questions are (1) Is there disclosure of how the planner is compensated? (2) Is the client given a choice? and (3) Does the planner have the personal integrity to deal with the conflict of interest? Because group 3 members are compensated based on transactions, they are the ones that are taking most of the flak in the general and financial press. However, since most of the writers do not understand the classifications listed, everyone gets painted with the same brush. Is the flak deserved? Some of it. However, like most issues, there are two sides.

Should timing and stock picking be "blessed" then by the financial planning community? Perhaps not, but I don't believe it should be condemned as completely wrong. Human nature suggests that people are always going to demand timing from their advisors. They will go after the latest and best stock. They are willing to pay for the thrill of playing the game. When clients read about a stock that returned 1,000 percent or more in one year, it excites them. It looks like a great way to get rich quick. They want their advisors to feed them information so they can catch a ride on the next rising star.

The media feed this attitude. Even the most respected publications come out with short-term performance analyses and lead stories on the latest hot stock. The public should be warned that this is for entertainment value, not investment value. One writer summed it up rather well when he said, "I feel like the judge that allows certain evidence to be presented to the jury, and then I instruct the jury to pay it no mind."

Even my least wealthy clients often wanted to own stocks that they had read great performance stories about. Because of commissions on both the purchase and sale of the small quantities they wanted, it was often virtually impossible to realize a good return in exchange for the risk they were taking. Usually, I talked them into buying shares in a mutual fund that owned the stock they liked. Sometimes, they could not be dissuaded and I made the purchase for them. My justification? They wanted to enjoy having their own stock to follow in the morning papers; as long as we both knew they had made an informed decision, it was still their money and their lives.

Is there anything wrong with going for the big returns or trying to get rich quick? It looks painless and exciting. Why shouldn't we take a chance at reaching the gold ring? The billions of dollars that go into lotteries prove that millions of Americans see chance as the only way to reach true financial security. This is a free country. I would never advocate taking away that right. However, it is wrong to pursue these rising stars and the fast track to riches if that is the only method you are using to reach financial security. If it is the only method, there is a high probability that you are going to wind up broke. For most clients, these get-rich-quick opportunities are too risky to pursue with anything more than pocket change for an occasional lottery ticket or pull on a slot machine handle. Some clients, however, pursue financial freedom in a systematic and sensible fashion with most of their available funds. They enjoy allocating a small portion of their funds toward investment gambling. Many have already attained or are close to attaining financial security and can easily afford to take an occasional fling at a high-flying stock. There is nothing wrong with either of these approaches as long as the investors are informed of the risks.

We have now separated financial consultants into three major groups. By the time you finish the remaining chapters, you should easily determine which group you desire to start in. Most of my experience is in group 2 financial planning combined with group 3 product sales. I have a bias toward that approach. You may enter the financial planning field working for someone in group 1, and that experience may lead you to group 2 or 3. The same could be said for the other groups. If you like the feel of having your "finger on the trigger" and watching the markets closely on a minute-by-minute basis with constant client contact, you may love group 3 or even group 1. If you prefer a more methodical approach with less-frequent client contacts over a longer period, then group 2 will be the place for you.

4

HOW CONSULTANTS
SELECT AND MANAGE
INVESTMENTS

One of the myths that I will explore later in this text is that financial planners' primary value stems from their ability to select investments. In chapter 3, I attempted to segregate financial consultants into three groups, while cautioning you that very few planners fit perfectly into any one group. Group 3 consists of people who sell products. Group 2 planners usually recommend people who manage money; however, they also often sell investment products. That happens partially because people who manage money often put their skills together in a packaged investment product. The most common of this type of product is a mutual fund. Mutual funds are investment companies formed to invest in a particular area of the economy or the economies of foreign countries, usually using a particular general type of investment (such as bonds or equities), with a particular type of outcome in mind. The consultants' job is to first determine what type of outcome clients have in mind, then find the products that offer the best chance of producing those outcomes in the time the clients have.

Let's do another visual image that may clarify this issue. Imagine the financial plan as a treasure map leading to the top of our mountain. The road leading to the top of the mountain is winding and has lots of hills, valleys, and plateaus. Several sections of the road are missing, making the map look like a partially completed puzzle. The journey to the top of the mountain involves several separate trips (substitute spokes and ropes or goals here). Each trip has its own hills to ascend and valleys to cross. With your map (financial plan), you have drawn a line leading to each destination, but the line is missing pieces at certain critical junctions. You need a ladder here, a bridge there, a tunnel here, and so forth. These ladders, bridges, and other tools represent products or investments. Once the map is drawn, it usually becomes rather obvious whether a ladder or bridge is needed.

The question for financial consultants is where to get the ladder or bridge. Do the clients buy the parts and build the connectors themselves (individual stocks and bonds)? Do they buy ladders and bridges that are already built to size and specifications (mutual funds and other packaged products)? Or do they hire others to build and maintain the bridges according to the clients' needs (individual money managers)? If they decide to build, where do they go to buy the material? Do they have the engineering skills to build a bridge or a tunnel? Also, a tunnel will require more than just parts; clients may need other consultants to construct it (possibly an attorney). If they decide to buy bridges and ladders that are already built, there is good news and bad news for clients. The good news is that there will probably be 2,000 to 3,000 options available to meet their needs; the bad news is that they must select from that large number. For many financial planners, making that decision is a daunting task. It certainly was one of the biggest challenges for me.

SOLVING THE PRODUCT PUZZLE

At the point of product selection in the financial planning process, financial consultants split into more types. There may be all types in each of the three major groups.

Type 1   Active Timing Managers

The first type of consultants believes that they bring value to their clients by timing the market and selecting specific investments, including packaged products. I call this type the *active timing managers*. They are money managers (group 1), people who recommend (select) money managers (group 2), and people who sell investment products (group 3). They engage in all the activities that place them in all three groups listed in chapter 3. These planners must be actively involved with their clients' investments on a daily basis. They must have current information at all times, because they have told their clients that they can bring value by telling them when to be in and out of equities, bonds, metals, real estate, and cash. Although they may sell packaged products where other people manage their clients' money, they select these products and money managers through a long analytical process. These consultants continually monitor their selections and their performances.

Type 2   Analytical Performance Managers

This type can squeeze blood out of numbers. They can quote statistics and name money managers from memory. If they can't remember the correct performance data, they have software at their fingertips that will tell them everything they need to know about any mutual fund, variable annuity, or traditional insurance product. This group differs from group 1 in that it does not consist of market timers. Consultants don't keep their fingers on the trigger. They generally are asset allocators and rebalance portfolios as the need arises. However, they are very picky about the products they choose. They are also usually performance oriented and expense ratio oriented. Although these planners talk publicly about past performance not being a good indicator of future performance, they privately believe that it is. They also believe that their particular analytical techniques will yield many more winners than losers. When giving a teaching seminar or writing articles about financial planning, they advise not to sell based on performance. In practice, however, they do just that. They quote performance statistics to their clients and believe that their primary value lies in their ability to pick winners.

Type 3   Asset Allocation Analysts

These consultants are very closely related to those of type 2 except they talk to their clients more about asset allocation and modern portfolio theory than they do about performance. They will also analyze the products ad nauseam looking for any imperfections. Asset allocation analysts may get hung up on one particular aspect of a product without looking at the entire picture. Expense ratios are the usual culprit. They are certainly concerned about performance but work more toward managing clients' expectations in accordance with investment policy statements specifically designed for clients. In other words, they try to keep risk at the clients' comfort levels while educating clients that high risk should yield high returns and low risk usually means lower returns. They also allocate assets according to the clients' time horizon. When short-term performance doesn't live up to expectations, this type of planner often must go back to square one with clients and talk about the value of asset allocation and long-term versus short-term thinking. Because they are so analytical, asset allocation analysts occasionally fall off the wagon and revert to type 2 when their methods do not work in the short term. Their methods often do *not* work in the short term, because they are specifically designed for the long-term investor.

Type 4   Nonanalytical Asset Allocators

These planners also believe in asset allocation and packaged products. They don't think that they can add any value for clients by trying to time the market. They do rebalance the clients' portfolios, but only as the need arises as a *result* of market changes not in anticipation of market changes. They also believe that most equity mutual funds of the same classification are generally the same. Nonanalytical asset allocators have done their homework on the products they use, but their analysis doesn't extend to the entire product universe. They believe that trying to analyze the universe is a nonproductive use of time. When they are choosing which products to build relationships with they concentrate on these principles:

1. They try to build relationships with product sponsors the same way they build relationships with clients. They want to be assured of superior service and informed about major changes in management. They want their problems handled quickly and smoothly. Nonanalytical asset allocators want the opportunity to be kept informed about the investment company through visits to the home office, telephone conference calls, private meetings, and meeting the people who are actually managing the money. They will remain loyal through short-term poor performance as long as they are kept informed about the methods being used and why the poor performance occurred. These consultants want competitive expense ratios but do not demand that a product have the lowest ratio in the marketplace. They realize that the entire package is more important than any single factor.

2. They try to weed out the bad guys but recognize that there are several factors to be considered before eliminating a product. Their analysis is usually based less on technical aspects than on relationship aspects. These planners try to get a feel for the company and its management. How they are treated ranks right up there with performance. The products that have basic flaws in concept, performance, management, expenses, or service are usually easy to eliminate.

3. Their analyses don't have to be all-inclusive. Nonanalytical asset allocators don't have to look at all the products before building a relationship, because their view of the product universe is different than the perspective of the first three types. They see most products as good and generally the same over time. Any differences usually converge or have less impact over long periods.

Types 1 through 3 see products very differently and bring their analytical skills to bear to discover the good and bad. They see allegiance to a small group of sponsors as a clear conflict of interest, and some even see type 4 planners as unethical or lazy.

Type 5   Buy-and-Hold Asset Allocators

These consultants are almost identical to type 4 planners in their view of products but adopt a more pragmatic approach to client relationships and asset allocation. They believe not only in the value of portfolio rebalancing but also that the benefits of rebalancing must be weighed against the costs. The costs of rebalancing include possible adverse tax consequences, client consternation and fear, time for the financial planner and client to analyze the consequences of rebalancing, additional tax preparation fees, and complexity added to both the planner's and the client's lives. They believe that most people want less complexity in their lives and not more. Also, for this type of financial planner, rebalancing implies timing and they can't stand the thought of it.

In fact, rebalancing does call for some timing. For example, what if you have had a large run-up in the market and your client is too heavily weighted in equities? As I write this, for example, we have had a bull market in 1995. If we follow the rules, we must rebalance by selling off some equities. But what if there is a larger bull market in 1996 or 1997? Our rebalancing will have been correct, but will the client appreciate the planner for not taking full advantage of a full year of a great bull market? In the long term, clients' risks are less when they rebalance, but they may have to take less in short-term performance. A good financial planner can handle this reeducation of clients and properly explain why their portfolios gained only 9 percent when the clients are reading about equity funds that returned 20 percent or more. A type 5 planner takes the pragmatic approach that "it all comes out in the wash" anyway, so why disturb the client?

Type 6   Analytical, Timing Salespeople

These salespeople often refer to themselves as stock or bond analysts. They frequently specialize in a particular type of product. How can you be an analyst and a product salesperson? You use your analysis skills on products. These people usually work for wirehouses and use the firms' research departments as their basis for analysis. They may focus on a group of stocks but usually concentrate on an industry or type of stock. They may also become bond specialists, tax-exemption specialists, or even mutual fund specialists. Analytical, timing salespeople also are timers. They use their own research and that of their firms to try to determine the direction of interest rates and the market. They believe that their educated guesses are far superior to the noneducated guesses of their clients as to where the economy and the markets are headed.

Type 7   Pure Salespeople

Pure salespeople usually have a stable of products that may include stocks, bonds, insurance products, or mutual funds. The products may change regularly, and selection may be based on their firms' research or consist of today's hot stock. They don't concentrate on building client relationships and certainly don't over analyze the product. They learn as much as they can and then start selling it. They want to sell a lot of their products. Most believe that there is a good chance the product will perform well for most people, but they are not going to spend much time trying to build a road map to see if it fits a particular client. They try to sell to more sophisticated investors who have the ability (at least they think they have the ability) to make the determination as to whether the product fits.

I have a grudging admiration for both types 6 and 7, even though the industry and press usually vilify their members. Just like all the other groups, there are bad apples. Because these groups are usually more aggressive, they may have more than their share. There are always a few who just want to peddle a product today, regardless of the consequences to the client. I believe that most, however, will sell only products designed to fit a need. They frankly tell clients that it is up to them to determine whether they have that need.

SELECTING YOUR TYPE

Which of the seven types should you be? It depends. Which of the three groups in chapter 3 appeals to you most? Do you want to be a money manager? If so, then you should probably lean toward one of the analytical types to start. This can be the analytical salesperson or one of the analytical planners. To be a good money manager, you must learn a lot about products and the nature of the markets. If you like the idea of building relationships as in group 2, you will probably pursue types 3, 4, or 5.

What type of planner am I? I come down squarely as a type 5. Although I believe and would like to practice more in the fourth type, my clients placed me in type 5. I like to build relationships with clients, but I like them to be comfortable and nonthreatening. I build road maps of all sizes and shapes. Some go to the top of the mountain and some to the first plateau. Some just untie a rope or two. I have very few clients who require or want active management. Because of taxes, fear, inconvenience, time constraints, or the size of the portfolio, most don't regularly rebalance. Since I do not take discretionary accounts, client meetings are necessary to rebalance. Most clients will not sit still long enough for me to inform them of the need to rebalance and to accomplish it.

I believe that selecting individual stocks and bonds is either recreation or gambling, not financial planning. For the wealthy client with "fun money" and extra disposable income, it can be appropriate; however, I believe that a majority lose money doing it. I base that opinion on what I read and on looking at more than 8,000 individual tax returns. For the less-than-wealthy or average client, actively trading stocks is just gambling. Trading costs and taxes will usually eat up most of the profits, if there are any.

I have neither the time, skills, nor inclination to try to time the markets. I like to simplify my clients' lives by helping them to realize their dreams and by giving them a trail to follow. I am ready to counsel them when events change the trail, but I don't like to change just so that I can say I am actively managing. I am not a money manager; I recommend people who manage money. I select products more on relationships than performance or expense ratios. I generally only have one rule when selecting a product: I stay away from short-term high performers. I rarely break that rule. I concentrate on minimizing loss rather than maximizing returns, because I believe that is what most of my clients want. They like high performance, but what they really want is to not lose money.

You won't see much written about type 5 consultants. Not many will admit to a pragmatic approach to financial planning. Some would say it is lazy. Not choosing from the universe of products and having "favorites" may be a conflict of interest. Not actively rebalancing may increase the clients' risks. I have an answer for every argument. Because of portfolio size, income level, time constraints, educational level, and personality traits, many people simply don't qualify to have their funds actively managed. Those in the profession don't want to talk about it, but many of the types preclude these clients from being served by quality financial planners.

Do these people need financial planning or should they be left to their own devices? I believe they need and deserve education about how to survive and prosper financially and have found that they appreciate guidance. Type 5 planning allows a financial consultant to serve these clients and still survive economically. To the purists, speaking of the financial planners' income may be politically incorrect. But if financial planners' are unable to make a profit in helping clients, they will not be practicing financial planning long. Everyone loses when planners' businesses don't survive. They often can't afford to spend a great deal of time with clients who have no money or a small amount to invest; however, using type 5 planning can help these clients.

As for the conflict of interest, I believe that most products of the same class are the same. I also believe that you either have integrity or you don't. If you don't, you will find a way to cheat in any of the groups or types. As for increasing risk by not rebalancing, I balance the risks against the disadvantages. For long-term investors, I have never been convinced that it doesn't "all come out in the wash." Remember, it is not a perfect world. Just as there are no perfect products, there are no perfect financial plans or perfect ways to practice financial consulting. I do not ask my readers or students to choose type 5. I also don't say that the other types are wrong. I think they all add value, and all have problems.

Your clients' needs or your own personal attributes may decide what type of planner you become. You may be able to practice partially in more than one group, but I think you will eventually practice primarily as one of the seven types. I think it would be foolish to begin as an analytical planner or a timer. If it is highly questionable whether an experienced consultant can add value in these areas, it is doubly so for beginning planners. Because the range of clients is broader and less sophisticated in this area, I highly recommend beginning in type 5 and letting your clients take you where you want to go. Alternately, many beginners start with wirehouses, go through their training programs, and begin as type 6 or 7 consultants. Let your clients and your own personal attributes decide. Do what you enjoy the most.

SELECTING THE PERFECT PRODUCT

The perfect product has the following attributes:

1. The highest current yield
2. The highest total return
3. No commission charge but is accompanied by a personal advisor who can be called for advice and consultation at any time without charge
4. Total liquidity
5. No risk
6. Tax free forever

As a financial planner, you will have many encounters with clients searching for the perfect product. I keep the previously mentioned attributes on my desk on a laminated sheet just to show these clients that I am prepared. When I ask them if this is what they are looking for, I will use a friendly tone to let them know that this product does not exist. Most people will easily accept this fact and reframe the direction of their search for the proper investment when I ask which of the traits of the perfect product are most important to them. Then the education process can begin. Always remember that clients are usually looking for guidance and the best deals they can get. You have to earn clients' trust by asking questions and listening to the answers. Then you can find the products that best suit their needs.

Making the Product Universe Smaller

Although many planners want to select from an entire universe, successful financial consultants usually narrow their list to a select few. My recommendation is to start with a few products and save yourself the agony of analyzing all of them. I think we all want to know that the entire universe is at our disposal but soon recognize that we cannot use it all. Just pick up some good horses for your stable that will consistently carry your clients where they want to go. My suggestions:

Select one to three mutual fund families to work with
Select one or two variable and fixed annuities

Select one to three insurance companies for traditional insurance products such as life insurance, disability, health, and long-term care.

If you can find quality products to meet your needs with one or two companies, then do so; however, most companies tend to specialize in a particular type of product.

Put Your Money Where Your Mouth Is

Always try to invest in the products you recommend. A wise client will ask you where your money is. It is reassuring for the client when you can show your own money invested in the product you are recommending. It is extremely difficult for ethical and competent advisors to sell products they would not invest in themselves. That doesn't mean that consultants have to own every product they recommend. It does mean that they *would* purchase the product if resources permitted or if their own situation were similar to that of their clients. I once had a very difficult time getting a fellow professional and close personal friend to invest his retirement savings through me. He eventually found a way to make himself comfortable with investment recommendations. He simply asked me what my retirement plan was invested in. When I showed him, he simply said "I'll have some of the same, please." Pretty smart, if you ask me.

BASIC TYPES OF PRODUCTS

Mutual funds are investment companies that design investment policies to attract investors with common goals and needs or to invest in a certain segment of the markets. Investors' money is pooled and invested according to the plan (prospectus). Investors' interests are stated in shares; values of the shares fluctuate daily. They have no definite maturity date.

   Tax exempts can be individual bonds, unit investment trusts, or mutual funds that invest in tax-exempt bonds; they are issued by tax-exempt organizations. Interest earned is exempt from income taxes and often from state and local taxes but is not always tax exempt for people receiving Social Security benefits.

Unit investment trusts are similar to mutual funds except that bonds contained in the trusts are not actively traded. They usually have definite maturity dates and prestated interest rates based on the holdings in the trusts. The trusts normally hold tax-exempt or taxable bonds.

Earnings on **annuities** are tax deferred until withdrawn. Annuities are sold by insurance companies and can be fixed or variable. Fixed annuities earn a stated interest rate, whereas variable annuities have several subaccounts that usually invest in mutual funds or with other money managers.

It is beyond the scope of this book to explain all the various types of **insurance products** available. You can obtain training on insurance through your broker-dealer, your insurance company, your general agency, or a professional training program. There is more to insurance planning than simply "buy term and invest the difference." Many products are specifically designed to provide liquidity at death, to insure the lives of partners in a business, and so forth.

MY FAVORITE INVESTING TECHNIQUES

I have previously discussed research strongly suggesting that diversifying your assets into various segments of the markets (**asset allocation**) will reduce your risk and increase your return over a long period. Based on this modern portfolio theory, several model portfolios have been constructed to fit clients' various risk tolerances, time horizons, income needs, tax brackets, and other specific goals. Each portfolio places a certain percentage of the clients' investments into these various components. Normal components might include

Growth funds (domestic)
Growth and income funds
Foreign stocks
U.S. government bonds
U.S. corporate bonds
High-yield bonds

Natural resources
Real estate
Tax-free bonds

Dollar cost averaging refers to investing fixed sums at regular intervals over time. When share prices rise, the fixed sum will purchase fewer shares. When share prices lower, the same sum will purchase more shares. This process will even out clients' costs per share.

I use both asset allocation and dollar cost averaging consistently with my clients. Like other investing techniques, they are not perfect. I have seen several articles attempting to prove that it is better to invest a lump sum than to dollar cost average. Of course, that is impossible to prove, because there are too many variables that make it impossible to make apples to apples comparisons. These variables include the type of investment being made, values at the time the lump sum was made, values when the investment was withdrawn, and period of investment.

Regardless of attempts to prove or disprove either method, I am convinced that they increase clients' comfort with their investments and decrease their risks. If my clients are comfortable, they are much less likely to do something in haste or withdraw their funds just after a decline in value. I admit that I like dollar cost averaging for another reason. Clients are often not aware of a major market drop. If they are aware, they can be easily comforted by a reminder that they will be buying more shares at a lower price. Purists could say that I am working with an attitude of "what clients don't know, won't hurt them." Perhaps. I prefer to say that not knowing may help clients.

FIVE MYTHS ABOUT FINANCIAL CONSULTING AND CONSULTANTS

Myth #1   The Financial Consultant's Primary Value to Clients

The perception is that a financial planner's only real value to clients is the ability to pick products, time the market, make complex technical analyses, and prepare book-length financial plans.

Many financial planners believe this. However, I have already shared my belief that most of us will never add value in *product selection*. Most clients' needs are simple, and simple needs are filled with simple products. If it takes me longer than one hour to understand the basics about a product, I will not sell it because it is too complicated. In my practice, I almost never mention a product by name to my clients until a decision has been made to implement the steps in the financial plan. To be a good financial planner, you don't have to analyze all the products in the universe. In fact, I don't believe it is possible to do that much research effectively and also run a financial consulting business.

Timing the market doesn't work. We can't add value there. If I knew where the markets were going, I would simply invest accordingly and wouldn't need to work.

Complex technical analyses are not required for most clients. Again, their needs are usually relatively simple. Most of my financial plans are prepared using a handheld financial calculator and word processing software. The learning curve in financial planning is relatively steep. Once you have prepared a few financial plans, you learn how to listen and to solve problems. Certainly, there will be occasions when a client has a complex technical situation. If you don't feel qualified to handle it, your network (discussed in chapter 6) will be there to assist you. Don't be afraid to seek help when you need it.

Book-length financial plans are not required for every client. In fact, they are very rare. Most clients will not read long plans. They pay the financial planner to make their lives simpler and better, not to complicate them. The majority of my clients would not sit still for a complete financial plan at first; they saw the way to the top of the mountain only after I had prepared a couple of partial plans. Even when I prepare a complete financial plan, my major task is to simplify it for the client. I prepare a summary up front and conclusions and recommendation summaries at the end.

If this myth about financial planners is false, what is the value of consultants?

1. Financial consultants help clients to discover their hopes, dreams, and aspirations. One of the most valuable skills of

a good financial planner is the ability to ask good questions and listen to the answers. Strange as it may seem, most people do not know where they are going in their financial or personal lives. Discovering where they want to be will improve all aspects of their lives.

2. Financial planners *guide* clients in taking steps toward their dreams. They prepare financial plans and discover and discuss fears and obstacles with clients to help them see the way toward their goals.

3. Financial consultants undergo initial and continuous training about working with clients to reach financial security. They deserve to get paid for passing along what they have learned to their clients. They *educate* clients about finances including various types of investments, how the markets work, how compounding works, which investments have produced the best results over longer periods, how tax deferral works, and how to use retirement plans effectively.

4. Financial planners are paid for encouraging clients to do simple but meaningful things such as *changing from sporadic savers into regular investors*. Most people are sporadic savers. They are like people who go on yo-yo diets. Clients put money into savings accounts for a period, then take it out. Planners teach them that they must invest both money and time. They learn the advantages of having long-term perspectives rather than looking for immediate gratification. Clients learn the difference between yield and growth and how growth is needed to offset the effects of inflation.

5. Financial consultants *explain* the different types of *risks* to their clients. A realistic client will understand that all investments contain some type of risk. Without the aid of a financial planner, most people overlook the most prevalent risk of all—the loss of purchasing power through inflation. Using a few comparisons of prices during the last 20 or 30 years, the financial consultant can easily illustrate this risk. After consulting a quality financial planner, clients will understand that risk flows with rewards: the lower the risk, the lower the reward that can be expected. Consultants

teach clients simple things about investing such as the importance of maintaining *emergency funds*. They also teach them about the value of *diversification* and how putting their eggs into different baskets can reduce their risk of breakage and help them save more eggs.

6. Financial planners help clients to *protect* the *assets* they have accumulated by analyzing their exposure to risk and determining that they have the proper kind and amount of insurance coverage. They also assist in selecting the proper form for conducting business and in designing trusts and other legal entities to properly protect clients.

7. Financial consultants assist clients in arranging for the orderly *transfer* or control of assets in the event of death or disability. Often, simply adding a clause to a will or trust can save as much as $250,000 in estate taxes. Electing to set up living trusts can provide for clients' possible incapacity or disability, which may save thousands in court costs and attorneys' fees.

8. Financial planners are great *coaches and counselors*. They are there when clients are ready to stray off course or sell when the market is down. They manage the clients' perceptions about return and risk. They reeducate clients who are bombarded with incorrect information and become fearful. They keep clients off the bench, in the game, and on track.

Myth #2   Average Americans Will Pay Professional Rates for Financial Planning

Most people are not wealthy (at least 95 percent of the population). At least 75 percent of Americans have never consulted a financial advisor and have no plans to do so. They do not see themselves as clients of financial consultants. When people are asked to pay for consultation by the hour, most will not do it because although they need financial planning they do not see it as an emergency or necessity. Clients will not remove money from their current bank accounts and put immediate stress on their lifestyles in order to enhance the wealth of financial planners.

How do they then avail themselves of the services of financial planners? How do consultants make them viable, economically feasible financial planning clients? I discovered that clients will pay for financial consulting when the money is taken from funds already set aside for savings or investment or from future investments, because there is no immediate threat to their lifestyle. Think about it. If you were asked to write a $1,500 check for a financial plan today, what would you think? Most people first wonder about the amount of money in their checking accounts. Do they even have enough money to cover the check? If they pay it out of their current checking accounts, how will they meet the remaining obligations they have for the month?

I believe that any financial planner who wants to offer consulting services to this 75 to 90 percent of the market will offer various methods for getting paid. When I offered my clients alternate methods of paying me, 90 percent chose commissions. Although there is a lot of press today about the trend toward fee-based planning, I think the term *fee based* is misunderstood. Fee based can include time-based or asset-based fees. I also think the trend may be overstated. According to the National Endowment for Financial Education CFP Survey of Trends, the percentage of planners paid *strictly* by commission was 26 percent in 1988 and 27 percent in 1995. Those paid strictly by fees were 19 percent in 1988 and 18 percent in 1995. Forty-two percent said they were paid by fees and commissions in 1995 compared to 55 percent in 1988. The other 13 percent were either paid by salary or salary plus commission. These numbers don't show a major trend toward fee-based financial planning. They do suggest that the financial consulting profession and the press may have created a trend that clients don't know about because they are not participating. Many industry leaders love to talk about the trend, want it to develop, and may even see it happening in their own practices. Nonetheless, I don't believe that most financial planners can steer their average clients away from commissions. The key is to give clients choices and fully disclose how you are going to get paid. Most people are not adverse to paying for financial planning services, they just need to know how they are going to pay and what value they are going to receive in exchange for their money. I will discuss more about how financial planners get paid in chapter 8.

Myth #3   Financial Consultants Don't Have the Integrity to Deal with Conflicts of Interest

The public reads a lot about how planners have a vested interest in selling them a product. The press tells people to avoid planners who take commissions, which is one of the reasons I think the trend data may be flawed. Many planners who take commissions are almost afraid to admit it when asked and elect not to respond when they are given the option. I think they are still the quiet majority. I also think that most of them would never sell an unsuitable product to a client simply because it had a larger commission than a more appropriate one. Putting aside ethics, integrity, regulations, and strength of character, doing so would be just plain stupid. Why jeopardize a profitable long-term relationship for a few more coins up front?

Sales of products or services often involve conflicts of interest. The opportunity to sell a higher-priced product or service is almost always there. There were many tubes put in children's ear when ear drops may have worked just as well because the operation is safe and profitable. Do you believe a dentist ever did a root canal when only a filling was needed or that an attorney ever charged clients for "thinking about their cases" during a round of golf? CPAs commonly use the term *value-added billing* to describe adding amounts to bills based on enhanced knowledge: this is legitimate and acceptable, but the potential for abuse certainly exists. Again, it is not a perfect world. Why should people who sell investment products undergo this popular bashing? If you don't have the integrity (and the intelligence) to treat your clients fairly, then you shouldn't be in this business or in any other where you deal with money or people. A few instances of abuse do not justify painting the entire profession with the broad brush of sleaze.

Myth #4   Clients Should Always Seek Out Consultants Who Don't Deal with Any Products

I have taught seminars to financial consultants for more than eight years. Many of the participants are CPA financial planners who practice time-based, fee-only financial planning. They do not implement their own financial plans either because they feel it is beneath them or they are not allowed to do so by rules of the profession in their states. Those planners always inundate me with questions about products. They are starved for information about one of the most important stages of the financial planning process—implementation. Financial planners who elect not to dirty their hands with commission-based products deprive themselves and their clients of more than two-thirds of the available investment products. They also deprive themselves of great opportunities for training about financial planning, the economy and markets, and the products themselves.

Can you think of many products that don't need some type of marketing and distribution system? Commission-based products use financial consultants as the primary component of their marketing and distribution systems. There is certainly nothing wrong with no-load products that market themselves through advertising and other direct-sale methods. However, when financial planners limit themselves to these products, they are often on the same level for information as their clients. There is usually no advanced level of information flow to planner than to their clients. Relationships are harder to develop in this environment, and thus problems may be harder to solve. When disaster strikes or emergency action is required, planners who have built strong relationships with products will be in a better position to act quickly on behalf of their clients.

Myth #5   Financial Planners Can Be Successful Selling Products They Wouldn't Buy

I know that there are always exceptions to this rule and that there are great product peddlers, stock-jockeys, and smile-and-dialers who can unload a lot of product they wouldn't personally touch. However, I think that brand of selling is going the way of the dinosaur. Some people may continue there, but not many will survive.

Why have I included these myths? Because I labored under them for the first two or three years I was in the profession. I was taught some of these myths by leaders in the profession and in academic studies. Even after I started discovering the reality behind each myth, I doubted my new information because I kept hearing the myths repeated and seeing them in print. Question these myths and see what you find in your career. If your common sense and personal experience tells you that some information you have received is wrong, it probably is, no matter what its source.

I hope I have given you enough information to be comfortable with products. Obviously, this is not intended to describe all products or product types. However, you should now know how financial planners work with products using different techniques to achieve the same desired result. You have a base to build on. Once you understand the basics and accept that the search for the perfect (or even the best) product is futile, your learning process will be accelerated. Gaining product knowledge will continue as long as you are a financial consultant because new products are developed daily.

5

MEETING THE BASIC REQUIREMENTS FOR ENTRY INTO FINANCIAL PLANNING

How does one gain entry to this profession? How do you gain the respect of your peers? How do you get other people to respect and seek out your advice? In this chapter, I will discuss the various doorways that lead to becoming a qualified, respected financial planner. I describe the tests that you need to take and the professional designations you should pursue. Although studying and following academic routes to specialized knowledge are important, remember that common sense, experience, and people skills are your best resources. I will consider the regulatory licenses and registrations first, followed by the optional professional designations.

It is difficult to really practice financial planning without being licensed with at least one regulatory authority. Even though I have discussed my antiregulatory position, I think that it is proper that anyone recommending investments be subject to some rules and laws. The two primary regulatory organizations are the Securities and Exchange Commission (SEC) and the National Association of Securities Dealers (NASD). Each state usually has a state securities board and a state board of insurance. I will refer to these groups as regulatory agencies. In addition, most financial consultants will want to affiliate with at least one professional group that allows entry only after meeting certain qualifications, usually including passing a tough exam. I will not attempt to write a definitive work on all the complexities and rules regarding the regulatory agencies, various tests, and rules of all the professional organizations and designations. However, I will give you enough information to make an informed decision as to which licenses and designations you should pursue and in what order.

REGULATORY LICENSES

Registered Representatives

Registered representatives are often referred to as stockbrokers, investment counselors, investment representatives, or account executives. All registered representatives have passed at least one test, and in most states two tests, that allow them to sell securities to the public. In order to take the tests, you must be sponsored by a broker-dealer. The broker-dealer will set up your tests and agree to supervise your activities after you become licensed. After selecting a broker-dealer to be your sponsor, you submit an application to that broker-dealer called a U-4 form, which is similar to an employment application. If the broker-dealer and the NASD approve your application, you then select which tests you wish to take. The tests are usually administered by an independent testing service. They are taken on a computer at the testing service facility, and results are known within minutes after the test is finished. All can be taken in less than one normal workday. Study materials are available directly from the broker-dealer or a training company that specializes in study materials for the exams. You can choose study materials, including practice exams, on computer disk or hard copy.

Series 6 or Series 7 Tests

If you believe that you will be selling only mutual funds and possibly some annuities (you also need an insurance license to sell annuities—more about that later) or certain qualified government securities, then the Series 6 test could be your best choice. It requires less preparation and time to take. However, it covers only a limited selection of products. If you are going to be a full-time financial planner with full qualifications, you must take the larger exam, Series 7. The other tactic is to take the less-threatening Series 6, then add the Series 7 or various other tests to sell specific products as the need arises.

I highly recommend the Series 7 test as appropriate for most people who take financial planning seriously and want to get on the quickest and best track to providing complete consulting services for their clients. Most of your competition will have taken the Series 7 exam. This test allows you to sell virtually any product that you will ever want to or have the need to sell in a normal financial planning practice.

Although the Series 7 test is intimidating to many, I usually recommend it over Series 6 and several other tests. However, there is one caveat. I have previously advised aspiring financial consultants to take the Series 7 exam, only to have them fail the test one or more times. After passing the Series 6 exam on the first attempt, they had a sense of victory and accomplishment and went on to become great financial planners. Most planners usually took the Series 7 test later. I mention this caution to show that there is no sure-fire advice as to which test to take to gain entry into the profession. Consider your timetable, your test-taking ability, and any other relevant factors and then make an informed decision that suits your personal situation.

Series 63 Test

Commonly referred to as the "blue sky" test, this exam is much less complicated and time-consuming than either Series 6 or Series 7 tests. It covers the various regulations and laws of the state where you are going to practice, as well as national laws of the securities industry as a whole. In almost all states, this exam is required in addition to the Series 6 or Series 7 test in order to be a registered representative.

Again, all of the previously mentioned tests are administered by an independent testing service with locations in all the major cities throughout the country under NASD rules and regulations. All tests can be completed in one day and are taken on computer. You know the results soon after you finish.

After passing the Series 6 or 7 and the Series 63 exams, you have met the testing requirements to become a registered representative of a broker-dealer. There are certain other forms to be completed for your broker-dealer and the NASD, but these tests are the primary barrier to entry. In addition to the U-4 form mentioned earlier, you must also be fingerprinted for background checks by the FBI. The fingerprints are kept on file to use in tracing you if you happen to abscond with someone else's money. Depending on the broker-dealer's particular requirements, there could be other background and history checks or minimum training courses before you are allowed to start. If you intend to supervise other registered representatives in a branch office, the Series 24 principal's license will usually be required. It may also be required if you work directly for a broker-dealer.

Selecting a Broker-Dealer

You do not have to be a registered representative to be a financial planner. However, I consider an affiliation with a broker-dealer one of the most important decisions you will make in your financial planning career. Most financial consultants practicing today are or have been registered representatives. Affiliation with a broker-dealer opens up a vast network of relationships with mutual funds, insurance companies, clearing firms, training firms, and experts on taxation, retirement plans, financial planning, and other subjects relevant to the profession. Many broker-dealers have proprietary software that is available to their registered representatives. People in the office of the broker-dealer can be tremendous resources for information about the profession in general, as well as particular client situations.

If you are new to the business, don't expect broker-dealers to fall all over themselves asking you to affiliate with them. They actively solicit people who are proven producers; few go after beginners. There are many firms that actively solicit members of other professional groups such as lawyers or CPAs because these people already have clients or professional credibility, but few recruit those who have no clients and are new to the profession. Don't let that deter you. Most will still welcome a serious candidate who is committed to being successful in financial planning.

Choosing a broker-dealer can be time-consuming and difficult. Most written advice I have seen on selecting a broker-dealer involves more time and expense than is practical for a beginner. My best short-cut advice is to select a broker-dealer the same way I recommend selecting a financial planner. Look for someone you feel good about. Try to identify a firm with which a long-term relationship feels comfortable. Examining relationships and objectiveness are my top criteria.

Examining Relationships If you already know people in the profession whose opinions you respect, talk to them first. Ask about their affiliations and their recommendations for your particular situation.

Talk personally with the people you will be working with, including back-office personnel who will be handling trades, solving problems, and paying commissions. If the broker-dealer has a branch office or office of supervisory jurisdiction system, then you may be working directly under a branch manager. This branch manager may be called a regional vice president or some similar title. You certainly want to personally visit with that branch manager and other people associated with the branch. They will be your primary source of contact with the broker-dealer. If there is no branch office system, ask who your primary contact will be at the home office and visit extensively with that person. If you are a beginner in the profession, most of the early interviews can take place over the phone. When you narrow your list down to one or two broker-dealers, I highly recommend visiting the home offices and speaking with your key contacts in person.

Ask for a list of other registered representatives in your area or representatives who started out in similar situations to your own with the firm. Contact the people listed and ask them to give you a frank appraisal of the firm. Ask for names of people who started with the broker-dealer under consideration but then left. Contact them and find out why they left. There is a danger that the firm will give you only highly satisfied representatives, but it is more likely that it will be objective. If you ask tough questions of most representatives, they will respond truthfully. Weigh both criticism and praise.

When you have narrowed your list to one or two broker-dealers, ask about top management. What are their backgrounds and lengths of time with the firm? Most firms will have written information about this. Then ask to personally interview the president or CEO. Find out the mission of the firm, future projections, and so forth. If top management does not have time to speak to you, it is not necessarily enough to cross a firm off the list, but it's definitely a negative sign.

Objective Criteria   Broker-dealer evaluation surveys. Financial Planning, Registered Representative, and a few other magazines have frequent broker-dealer comparison surveys. Ask the firms you are working with for copies of these surveys. Pay special attention to criteria that are scored high or low and ask for explanations. These surveys are also good places to start looking for a broker-dealer. However, many firms do not participate; that is not an indictment of the firm. You can still use the list to ask more probing questions.

Training. Training should be one of the most important considerations for the beginning representative. Be sure to find out whether the firm provides orientation training for the new representative. Be especially wary of home office personnel who take a condescending attitude toward representatives who are new to the business. You don't want to be hammered every time you ask a question; you need counseling and advice. Find out if there is a training curriculum. That is, is there an organized approach to training so that all facets of financial planning are eventually covered? Who conducts the training and how much experience do they have? When and where is the training conducted and what is the cost to you? Are there firm-wide conferences held at least annually? Ask to see some sample training materials.

Product selection. Product selection continues to be one of the primary considerations for representatives when selecting or remaining with a broker-dealer. I find that a little difficult to understand because most independent broker-dealers handle almost all the same products. You need to find a firm with a wide product list in mutual funds, fixed and variable annuities, and unit investment trusts. You also need to take a close look at its approach to insurance. What are the companies, what are the types of products, and how is support handled? Is there a preferred product list as well as a comprehensive list? If so, is there a payout difference on the preferred list? Will you be paid less for selling products not on the preferred list? Does the firm manufacture its own products? Will you be pressured to sell them?

Payout. Ask for a copy of the payout schedule. This will show the percentages of payout on various types of transactions. For example, if the gross commission on a particular mutual fund is 4 percent, a $100,000 purchase would yield a gross concession of $4,000 (disregarding break points on commissions for which larger purchases result in lower commissions). Broker-dealers will keep anywhere from $200 (a 95 percent payout) to $3,000 (a 25 percent payout) of the gross $4,000—a huge difference. However, the highest payout doesn't always equal the best broker-dealer. There are certain basics about gross margins in the business that bring all payout schedules fairly close when all factors are considered. Some firms, for example, make up for higher payouts by charging high transaction costs. Others will provide a lot of overhead support such as office rental, secretaries, or research in exchange for a lower payout. You usually get what you pay for, but you need to decide what is worth paying for. What are the services you want and how valuable are they to you? You don't want to pay for services through lower payout or high fees if those services have little or no value to you. I like payout schedules that reward productivity and treat everyone equally. I don't mean equal payouts for everyone but equal opportunities to reach the highest payout and not having to negotiate to see who can get the better deal. I don't want to be having dinner with a fellow representative and find out she produces 50 percent less than I do but receives 10 percent more payout.

Financial condition. Ask to see comparative financial statements. If the company is sustaining losses or declining revenues, ask for an explanation. Look at its current ratio. Current assets should exceed current liabilities by about 1.5 to 1. In my opinion, failure to meet these criteria does not take the firm out of contention. Even if the firm is privately held and will not release financial reports, that would only be one factor in my decision. Financial condition, although important, is not as critical as a prospective representative might believe, because the firm usually does not keep clients' money for more than 24 hours. A more critical question might be what insurance the firm carries to cover possible losses of client funds. Ask for the total coverage, per case coverage, and an analysis of how the coverage relates to the size of the firm. I am not giving precise numbers to look for, because it depends on the size and nature of the firm's business.

Other good questions:

What is the clearing firm used by the broker-dealer? Very large firms will often do their own clearing. How strong is the relationship? What is the satisfaction level among representatives and back-office staff? Ask some representatives this question directly.

What methods does the home office use to communicate with the representatives? Are there newsletters, operations manuals, marketing manuals, and training manuals?

What ancillary relationships does the firm have? Is there a list of trust companies, attorneys, and so forth that have been subjected to due diligence?

Will I have minimum production requirements? This is not usually absolutely crucial, but it is an important issue. If the firm has no production requirements, you may be associating with a peer group that is not successful. Ask about average production. If a firm's minimum production is a problem, you may want to reconsider.

What type of insurance coverage does the firm offer? What is the professional liability or errors and omissions coverage? Is it mandatory for all representatives? How much will it cost? Mandatory coverage will usually insure the lowest rate for all participants. If you do not wish to carry it, however, or have insurance from another source, it could be a problem.

How will you be treated if you elect to leave the firm? Changing broker-dealers is not easy or pleasant. It can be excruciating if the original broker-dealer does not cooperate by granting blanket transfers of your clients' portfolios. Some broker-dealers consider the clients their own; if you leave, the clients stay and are assigned to another broker with the firm. You want a firm that will agree to blanket transfers of your accounts if you leave.

These are not all the factors to consider when choosing a broker-dealer. However, most people cannot practically examine every factor for every broker-dealer under consideration. Just concentrate on the ones that are most important to your long-term future. Resist the temptation to go for short-term gratification rather than long-term relationships. It is much better to select a broker-dealer for life, so look closely. The decision can and should be reversed if it was the wrong one, but it is very inconvenient and sometimes painful and expensive.

Insurance Licenses

The second type of license that should be pursued by financial planners is insurance. Many financial planners new to the profession balk at the notion of getting licensed to sell insurance. Given the industry's tainted reputation, I can understand this view. However, if you have reduced your beliefs about insurance to include only negative aspects, you need to rethink your position. Insurance is part of the financial planning process.

You do not have to sell insurance in order to include it in clients' financial plans, but I highly recommend that you be capable of doing so. The insurance test is not terribly difficult in most states, but the bureaucratic process of applying to take the test can be cumbersome, with long delays. If you find yourself in a position in which action needs to be taken for clients, you don't want to have to wait weeks or months to get licensed to properly handle your clients' needs. I have seen this happen many times in training financial planners who were licensed registered representatives but not licensed for insurance. A need for insurance or an annuity became evident in a client's financial plan, and an insurance agent had to be called to handle the transaction. This takes money away from financial consultants, requires that clients transact business with another party with whom they may or may not be comfortable, and makes it difficult for financial planners to track future activities in the insurance product sold.

I am not ruling out the advantages of bringing in insurance experts to assist in financial planning, but you should not have to depend on another professional in every situation. Under the team approach, planners bring in experts in the various disciplines such as securities brokerage or insurance so that all of the clients' needs can be addressed by experts in each area. This sounds very good on the surface, but I practiced it for several years with disastrous results.

Working with a team of *experts* sounds very good in theory, but I found it did not work well in practice. Many factors contributed to the difficulty. For example:

> *Who is going to be the team leader?*   As the financial planner, it is easy to think that this position naturally falls to you. Not so. The leadership position may change depending on the subject being discussed. If you put together a team of true experts, then you are going to have some strong personalities on your team. If the subject being discussed in a team meeting falls under one individual's area of expertise, she can easily assume the mantle of leadership. Her leadership may or may not please you. Also, some of the experts may simply relate to the client especially well. The client may defer to that natural affinity. I found that I had to earn my position of leadership, even when I called the meeting and brought the client. I didn't find earning my position too difficult, but I did find controlling my colleague's subsequent relationships with my clients to be impossible. In describing these control problems, I often use the analogy of a football team. As quarterback of the team, you call the plays. Ever try to tell an attorney to go out for a pass? Stockbrokers and insurance agents will be excellent team players in the short term—anxious to cooperate with you. Often, however, they would contact the client again without my knowledge and sell products that I had not recommended. In at least one situation, this resulted in my losing the client.
>
> *Unfair distribution of compensation.*   Most financial consultants who use the team approach are fee-only advisors. I was a fee-for-service advisor when I used this approach.

As a result, I was usually the lowest paid member of the team. I am not talking about small differences in compensation. Most team situations result in inverse relationships of reward and effort. The team member who does the least amount of work often is the highest paid.

Economic and time constraints. Putting together teams is awkward and very time-consuming. Huge blocks of time were absorbed trying to simply coordinate the schedules of the various members and the client. Several meetings are usually required. This can lead to a huge expense for the client or make the whole engagement economically unfeasible for the planner or other team members. Worse, the client can become frustrated with the entire process and stop the implementation.

Even if you use the team approach and want to use insurance consultants, it never hurts to be licensed. Often, your insurance license and affiliation with certain companies will be the only glue that holds a deal together.

Still have doubts about being licensed? What if your client's situation calls for placing $250,000 in a variable annuity? Assume further that the variable annuity is the only investment vehicle that will achieve the investment goals the client has detailed for you? What if the client is very resistant to fees—either time based or asset based? The only compensation lies in the only solution on the table—the commission from the variable annuity (probably around $10,000 gross). Do you want to give that to the insurance agent who can't share it with you because you are not licensed? Did the agent earn it or did you?

How do you get licensed for selling insurance? There are several methods that vary from state to state. All are relatively easy to accomplish, aside from the bureaucracy. As in the case of broker-dealers having to sponsor you for NASD exams, an insurance company must sponsor you for the insurance exam in most states. If you are already licensed as a registered representative, your broker-dealer should take you through the process and find an insurance company to sponsor you. If your broker-dealer does not provide these services, you need to contact an insurance company or agent on your own to be your sponsor for the exam. This exam is usually administered by computer and can be taken in less than one day. Study materials for the exam can be obtained from several sources. Your broker-dealer will usually have its own study materials or relationships with training firms that supply the materials.

Registered Investment Advisors

The registered representatives previously discussed are supervised directly by their broker-dealers and indirectly through the NASD's supervision of their broker-dealers. The SEC also gets involved in indirect supervision of representatives through the broker-dealers and their clearing firms. Thus, there are at least two agencies supervising the registered representatives, along with their own broker-dealer's direct supervision. When representatives make transactions for clients, the transactions must be submitted to the broker-dealer along with account applications for the clients. These applications detail critical information including net worth, investment experience, risk tolerance and other data. This information allows broker-dealers to determine whether investments are suitable for the clients. All of these rules and regulations are written and enforced for clients' protection.

Now consider the role of a financial planner who is not a registered representative but who is recommending investments to clients. Planners may be assisting clients in purchasing no-load mutual funds that do not have to go through a broker-dealer. They may be making recommendations that clients can implement themselves or through others. Where is the supervision in these situations? Not the broker-dealer, because there is none. Not the NASD because there is no broker-dealer involved with this planner. Not the SEC, because the planners' names may not show up anywhere in relation to a traded security.

Here's another example. What about financial planners who are registered representatives but are also recommending for clients investments that do not have to be purchased through the broker-dealer? The representatives could be recommending individual money managers, no-load funds, or other products that don't directly connect to representatives or their broker-dealers. Broker-dealers, although required to supervise all of the activities of their registered representatives, may not be informed because there is no account application to judge suitability. There is no supervision in either case.

The registered investment advisor was created to bring these planners under supervisory control. Registered investment advisors are licensed by and registered with the SEC and the appropriate state securities board. The SEC requires an extensive application and a fee that is currently $150. Some states require an exam—the Series 65, Uniform Investment Advisors Exam. Registered investment advisors are subject to periodic random audits by the SEC or state securities boards. Some states require the certified financial planner or similar designation before licensing an investment advisor.

Most registered investment advisors advise clients for time-based or asset-based fees. Their recommendations may include investment products that are either purchased through another source or that do not have to go through a broker-dealer. Many registered investment advisors may fall into the group 1 category of people who manage money; that is, they may actually actively manage portfolios for clients. If fees are asset based, advisors' incomes are based on a percentage of the clients' portfolios. These percentages usually range from one-quarter of 1 percent to 2.5 percent. If fees are time based, clients are charged by the number of hours the financial consultants spend on their clients' financial matters. Some may also charge based on the function performed. For example, a financial plan might have three different rates ranging from $450 to $5,000. These fees are still time based.

Should you become a registered investment advisor? If you are going to perform any of the functions just described, you must. If you are affiliated with a broker-dealer, that broker-dealer will probably be a registered investment advisor. You can register as an agent of the broker-dealer's registered investment advisor. That is probably the cheapest and best route to take. Any activities regarding investment counseling, financial planning, investment recommendations, and so forth must be reported and approved by the broker-dealer.

PROFESSIONAL DESIGNATIONS

The financial planning profession is an alphabet soup of credential initials. According to the North American Securities Administrators Association (NASAA), about 30 organizations offer some kind of designation for investment advisors and financial planners. (Maybe we need a regulation to stem the tide of professional designations.) Depending on which organization or individual you talk to, theirs is the designation of choice.

I am a CPA (certified public accountant), CFP (certified financial planner), and CLU (chartered life underwriter). I also qualified as a member of the International Association for Financial Planning's Registry, before that title was discontinued. In an agreement between IAFP and the CFP organizations, Registry members were granted CFP status after meeting a few additional requirements. Those who already had the CFP simply lost a designation in that exchange. This profession loves initials. I took a rather difficult test and met some other requirements to become a member of the Registry, including getting testimonials and references from clients. I mention this to show that you can overcredentialize. When you have all those initials, each set has its own set of continuing education requirements. Some overlap, but each requires a report. Each has annual fees and an associated professional group that also has membership dues. You can get involved in too many professional associations.

To help you make a decision as to the professional credentials you want to pursue, I am providing some basic information on each. This may not be all inclusive, because new initials emerge regularly.

Certified Financial Planner (CFP)

Currently, approximately 79 colleges have registered with the Certified Financial Planner (CFP) Board of Standards to provide the pretesting course work for this designation. The CFP Board is a professional regulatory organization acting in the public interest by establishing and enforcing education, examination, experience, and ethics requirements for CFP licensees. It is responsible for testing and certifying CFP candidates. You can participate in one of the approved financial planning course work programs that consist of ten classes. If you hold a CPA designation or MBA or law degree, you can challenge the comprehensive exam without course work. Alternately, you can do self-study and take the ten-hour comprehensive exam. The comprehensive exams include foundational information about financial planning, the financial planning process, insurance, investments, income tax, retirement planning and employee benefits, and estate planning. The exams are given every January and July. The tuition is currently $1,995. You will also have to meet some minimum experience requirement before using the CFP designation. Contact the National Endowment for Financial Education (NEFE), 4695 South Monaco Street, Denver, Colorado 80237-3403 (303-220-1200) for more information. The NEFE serves as an umbrella organization for the College of Financial Planning, Institute for Tax Studies, Institute for Wealth Management, Institute for Retirement Planning, and NEFE Public Education Center.

I think that most professionals in the industry would say that the CFP is the most widely recognized of the industry designations. "The CFP has become the designation of choice of serious financial planners from wirehouse reps to CPAs," says Bob Clark in the July 1995 issue of *Investment Advisor* magazine. Similarly, John Rubino, in *Your Money,* January 1995, suggests that "CFP is rapidly becoming the standard designation."

Chartered Financial Consultant (ChFC)

To earn the chartered financial consultant (ChFC) designation, you must complete the American College's ten-course program with tests after each program. Tuition is approximately $2,660. Halfway through the ChFC (five courses), you meet the qualifications to sit for the CFP exam. Founded in 1927, the American College in Bryn Mawr, Pennsylvania, offers the ChFC, CLU (chartered life underwriter), REBC (registered employee benefits consultant), and RHU (registered health underwriter) designations. The American College also recently registered with the CFP Board of Standards to provide the course work to sit for the CFP exam. According to John R. Driskill, of the American Society of CLU/ChFC, "The American Society is very enthusiastic about this development. In effect, it means if you are going to be active in financial counseling, you should obtain the CFP license. And if you really want to distinguish yourself as a financial counselor, you should earn the ChFC professional designation." Notice a little polite competition going on in that last sentence? If you're interested, the American College can be reached by telephone at 1-610-526-1490 or see Appendix A for more details.

American Institute of CPAs–Personal Financial Specialist (AICPA–PFS)

The AICPA has established a specialty designation program for CPA financial planners. The PFS designation program is exclusively for CPAs with considerable experience in personal financial planning who want to demonstrate their knowledge, skill, and experience by earning the credential. It is the first accredited specialty program established by the AICPA and is administered by the PFP division.

Candidates for the PFS designation must

1. Be a member of good standing of the AICPA
2. Hold a valid CPA certificate
3. Have at least 250 hours of experience per year in PFP activities for the three years immediately preceding the application.
4. Submit a written statement of intent to comply with all the requirements of reaccreditation. Reaccreditation occurs every three years and requires holders to show that they are actually practicing financial planning, still hold a valid CPA certificate, and so forth.
5. Successfully complete a six-hour written examination in personal financial planning.
6. Submit six references substantiating professional experience in personal financial planning.

The first four requirements must be met before sitting for the exam. References are required only after notification of passing the exam. The exam is offered at more than 300 exam sites twice a year. Applicants can obtain more information about the exam by calling 1-800-864-8080.

Chartered Life Underwriter (CLU)

Also offered by the American College, chartered life underwriter (CLU) is the designation of choice for most insurance professionals. I chose it because I wanted to have what I considered to be the premier designations for accounting (CPA), financial planning (CFP), and insurance (CLU). This is also a ten-course program with a test after each course. After obtaining this designation, two more tests will qualify you for the ChFC.

Chartered Financial Analyst (CFA)

Considered by many to be one of the toughest designations to achieve because of the highly technical nature of the comprehensive examination, chartered financial analyst (CFA) is probably the designation of choice for the people in group 1 (these who manage money). The education and tests cover the action of markets and the economy. Designation and tests are administered by the Association for Investment Management and Research, P.O. Box 3668, Charlottesville, Virginia 22903.

Certified Investment Management Analyst (CIMA)

Administered by Investment Management Consultants Association, the certified investment management analyst (CIMA) designation also requires a comprehensive exam, three years consulting experience on investment policy, and a prescribed course of study offered through the Wharton School of Business. Contact the IMCA at 9101 E. Kenyon Avenue, Suite 3000, Denver, Colorado 80237.

Certified Fund Specialist (CFS)

The institute of Certified Fund Specialists of La Jolla, California provides advisors with this comprehensive and practical mutual fund and annuity education and exam. By successfully completing the advanced Certified Fund Specialist program, advisors earn this designation. Tuition is approximately $750 and the institute can be contacted at 1-800-848-2029.

Chartered Mutual Fund Counselor (CMFC)

Not to be outdone by the CFS, the National Endowment for Financial Education teamed up with the Investment Company Institute to announce this new designation—chartered mutual fund counselor (CMFC)—in January 1996. Tuition is $750. The course includes nine modules that cover open- and closed-end funds, asset allocation, portfolio risk, and retirement planning.

Master of Science Degree Program

The College for Financial Planning now offers the master of science degree with an academic emphasis in financial planning. There are four crucial areas of study:

1. *Wealth Management* concentrates on investment strategies and portfolio management, professionally managed assets, real estate investment, and case studies in wealth management.

2. *Retirement Planning* covers financial planning for the retired, pre-retirement financial planning, qualified retirement plans, and case studies in retirement planning.

3. *Tax Planning* draws from a variety of functional areas and covers tax planning for owners of a closely held business, tax planning for the highly compensated, tax practice, and case studies in tax planning.

4. *Estate Planning* focuses on advanced estate planning techniques, estate and insurance planning for business owners, the use of trusts in estate planning, and estate planning case studies.

For more information, call 303-220-4800.

I know that I have not begun to cover all the professional designations that exist. I have discussed the ones I know something about and the ones that I think beginning financial planners may want to be familiar with. Obviously, there is a lot of duplication. Don't worry too much about the size of the elephant, just take one bite at a time. Be selective about what study program you enter and choose the one most applicable to your practice and the one that will yield immediate benefit to your clients. If I had thought in the beginning that I would eventually go for the CFP as well as the CLU, I probably would not have gotten involved. Get started in the business. Help clients. Ask questions. Then go for the appropriate designations. In chapter 8, I will offer my recommendations for the sequential order to getting licenses and professional designations. Those recommendations will be based on my personal experience as well as my interaction with and training of several financial planning colleagues.

6

GETTING CONNECTED TO THE PROFESSION

When I was practicing public accounting and financial planning in the small town of Commerce, Texas, it was easy to become a "joiner," even for an introvert. In a small town, your contribution is needed and appreciated. You can easily see how to make a difference by contributing your time and support. During the first five years of my practice, I didn't interact much with my own profession. When I entered financial consulting, the same was true. I just couldn't quite make the connection as to how interacting with my peer group (and my competitors) would benefit me and my clients. In my opinion, I was seeing more than enough of my colleagues at professional education meetings and conferences. I made no effort to go beyond taking the education courses that I needed to help my clients. I was getting plenty of continuing education so that I could stay current in my profession and provide the very best service possible for my clients. However, I didn't see the cost-benefit relationship correctly when I considered joining additional groups and becoming something other than a perfunctory member. I was satisfied with this situation in public accounting for several years. However, when I entered financial planning, I found that I could not get the training I needed from my usual sources for continuing professional education. When I decided to venture out to get some needed training, I found a nationwide network waiting for me. This network was mine for the taking and remains one of the best assets in my career.

Where did this network come from? Primarily it developed from the following four sources:

1. My broker-dealer
2. Product sponsors and service providers
3. Trade associations
4. Professional organizations

Although the connections overlap, it is important to explore each one for all the information, services, and contacts possible.

BROKER-DEALER CONNECTIONS

If you have done your homework in selecting a broker-dealer, that connection alone will put you on the path to almost all of the other connections. See Appendix B for information on becoming licensed as a Registered Representative of a broker-dealer. Your broker-dealer should be actively involved with the various trade associations. Management and staff at the broker-dealer should hold some or all of the designations that you aspire to. That means that they also belong to most of the professional organizations you want to become part of. However, I believe that the most important connection the broker-dealer provides is to product sponsors and service providers.

Effective Use of Product Sponsors

For our purposes, the term *product sponsors* includes all of the mutual funds, insurance companies, unit investment trusts, limited partnerships, trust companies, pension administrators, and other groups that sell various investments and services to financial planners. I have found them to be an invaluable resource for technical expertise, training, marketing, and general information about the profession. As a registered representative, you will have many opportunities to hear product sponsors speak about their products and services, the economy, and the profession as a whole.

Do not make the mistake of minimizing the value of what the sponsors say because they represent a certain product or company. You should have the confidence to segregate the wheat from the chaff. Most of their offerings will be wheat. Remember that a lot of these organizations manage billions of dollars for individuals and institutions. Most hire the very best in the profession. They have pockets deep enough to hire specialists and experts in all areas. They may have economists, portfolio managers, research specialists, retirement plans specialists, tax specialists, professional motivators, and trainers on staff. Many of the leading speakers in the nation work for these firms. I believe that you should limit your product selections as soon as possible (more on this later). Why not pick up some valuable information while going through the selection process?

I was surprised that the product sponsors would make their people and services available to me. Most of the services are free or very inexpensive. Of course, in exchange for these services, they want you to market and sell their services or products to your clients. There is nothing wrong with that: it is perfectly ethical to learn as much as you can from the various groups. You don't want to take advantage of product sponsors, but you can use their resources and information without being unfair. For example, it would be unethical to ask product sponsors to pay for a seminar for your clients when you have no intention of ever using their products. However, if product sponsors invite you to a group meeting where they will present their products or talk about retirement plans, the state of the economy, and so forth, you should feel free to attend as many of these meetings as possible. Never pass up the opportunity to learn something.

When I decided to really connect to the financial planning profession, I was impressed by the depth and quality of services these product and service providers placed at my disposal. I increased my Rolodex of telephone numbers by 20-fold. Listen to what each provider has to say. They will not only be talking about their products or services but also sales and marketing ideas, technical issues, and economic or investment issues.

Building an Expert Database

As you interact with professionals, you should immediately start building an *expert database*. I suggest starting with a three-ring binder with tabs for the various disciplines such as retirement plans, education funding, asset allocation, planning for the elderly, annuities, traditional insurance products, and estate planning. Each time you attend a meeting or hear a speaker from a group with expertise in any area, copy the business card on a big sheet of paper and put it behind the appropriate tab. If someone gave you excellent material on the subject, put that in the binder as well. Then, as you gather good information on any particular subject from any source, place the best of the information in the binder. You will soon need several books. Keep refining these books as you add to them. If you are like me, you will wind up with one for the expert database with nothing but business cards, addresses, and phone numbers. Another whole group will have technical information about the various disciplines. A third group may hold marketing information with binders for each type of information. My group grew to 35 binders and became a valuable resource, as well as the basis for two published books. In a very short time, you will have names and numbers to call for almost any question you may have. I am not implying that you should never have to do any research on your own, but having a qualified expert who specializes in a particular area of the profession to listen to ideas and questions is invaluable. That is the best type of research.

Due Diligence Trips

Many product sponsors will offer due diligence trips to their home offices so that you can meet the people who handle your accounts, portfolio managers, even members of top management. Those trips offer another opportunity to add to your growing network. Due diligence trips receive some negative press because of the perception that people who participate will feel pressured to sell the products because of the trips. However, I have taken dozens of these trips and found them all very professional. I see nothing wrong with an organization educating its customers about its products and services and simply putting its best foot forward. I have never been pressured to sell anything as a result of any of these meetings. I did, however, make valuable contacts that I later used for the benefit of my clients.

Alternate Distribution Systems

The investment and insurance companies that market their products through a sales force also get a lot of criticism from the press because the ultimate consumer pays a load or commission. What is seldom mentioned is that approximately 65 percent of the investment products available today are distributed in this manner. What may be more important is the training these organizations provide to the general public through financial planners. I don't know what the percentage is, but the best training I have ever received has come from these product sponsors. Most is information that would never reach the public without the planner distribution system. All products are delivered through some type of distribution system. That might be mail, telecommunications, and so forth. I find it very naive to believe that the general public is not well served by having financial consultants as an optional part of any distribution system for financial products or services.

Product Sponsor Seminars

Another great way to connect to product sponsors is through conferences, industry meetings, and seminars. Most product sponsors have qualified speakers on staff to present seminars for your clients. Although I believe it is preferable for financial planners themselves to be the primary speakers at client seminars, you may fear public speaking more than death. If so, having a product sponsor speak to your clients is appropriate. Even if you are a qualified speaker, it never hurts to have support, both financial and otherwise, when giving a seminar. Don't worry about the product sponsor getting up in front of your group and promoting a one-size-fits-all approach with your clients. Those days are gone. On the contrary, most can speak on almost any subject you wish to bring to your clients. Although they will want to give some mention to their products, they will do it in a very professional and nonthreatening manner. If you decide to use the products of a particular firm extensively, it may be possible to arrange a visit from a portfolio manager or the top economist from the firm to make presentations to your clients.

Attending Conferences and Training Meetings

Most broker-dealers who believe in training their representatives hold at least one conference each year. These conferences can be fun, exciting, and educational. It is almost impossible to measure the value of a particular conference. As a cost-conscious CPA, I was very aware of each conference fee that I paid, as well as the travel costs I incurred. I believe that almost every conference will deliver at least one idea or connection that will pay for all of the costs. If you pick up ten ideas and connections, the benefits are even greater. This shift in thought is another appropriate use of reframing techniques. Start thinking of the conference as an investment rather than an expense. A tenfold or better return on your investment is probable for each conference you attend.

Most conferences will have a mixture of motivational speakers, technical speakers, top producers, workshops, and so forth. There will also be great opportunities for networking. I have attended more than 50 of these conferences. I had direct responsibility for planning at least nine major conferences and numerous smaller gatherings; I was sensible enough to hire someone who had expertise in planning meetings and not interfere too much in what this expert did. We combined his experience in planning with mine as an attendee to try to produce the best conferences possible. According to participant evaluations, we have attained that goal. We will never reach perfection, but our efforts have been successful, partly because we seek input from the participants and act on their suggestions whenever possible. Most suggestions are valuable. However, I have observed that many people simply do not know how to attend conferences.

Are there really right and wrong ways to attend conferences? Probably not. However, there is a right way and a wrong way for each individual attending a conference and there are some common mistakes made by attendees. It has been my observation that many people do it backwards. Those who most need technical information are noticeably absent from the technical sessions; those who need help marketing are either absent or asleep in the marketing sessions. I know that I was a show-me attendee for many years. When I reframed my attitude and started looking for gems rather than stones at each conference, the conferences' value to my practice and my income increased tenfold. Here are some of the types of attendees I have observed and real remarks I have seen on conference evaluations.

The Show-Me Attendee

This label described me a few years ago. I arrived at the conference looking for faults. As an experienced conference attendee, I was all puffed up with my knowledge about conferences. I started spotting flaws the minute I arrived at the facility. After all, I had spent a lot of money and valuable time to attend this conference and wanted something to show for it. Any speaker who was not as good as Ronald Reagan was crucified in my evaluation. I found fault in most of the events, the facility, and the hotel or resort staff. I started collecting stones from the moment of my arrival and they made up the bulk of my conversations with attendees. I guess I didn't have much else to talk about, so I threw the stones around. Even with this silly attitude, I invariably picked up a few diamonds at even the worst conferences. I would never have admitted it at the time, though.

The Nitpicker

This type is a kindred spirit to the show-me personality but tends to be more detail oriented. This attendee fails to provide requested travel information or arrival times but is furious when not picked up at the airport. It goes downhill from there. She doesn't like the wallpaper in the rooms and the bellmen's uniforms don't fit and need pressing. The amenities in the room are the wrong brand. She uses a different shampoo at home and expected it to be in the room.

Let's Party

This person's only complaint is that there is never enough free time for networking and playing. The attendee is either smart and can't learn anything else or just came to have fun.

The Technician

This attendee believes it is a very complex and demanding profession and that we need more technical sessions and less eating, drinking, and fun activities. He wants the conference components to make the most of his time. He didn't attend to learn about marketing or selling and especially not to have fun.

The Nerd

Selling is illegal, immoral, and fattening, according to this attendee. The nerd asks speakers to refrain from ever mentioning their products and feels pressured during the entire conference.

The Salesperson

This attendee wants to cut out the technical stuff. She doesn't know what half the speakers are talking about. She needs to make more money. The salesperson only wants to learn how to market and sell.

The Timekeeper

The timekeeper complains that the meetings are not on time if one speaker runs over the time limit and throws everything off schedule. I am a timekeeper also; I hate it when the conference gets off schedule. However, sometimes it cannot be helped. When that happens, we all try to make up the time and make the best of the situation. Ironically, many complaints about time come from people who are chronically late in arriving and cause the meetings to be delayed.

The Escape Artist

This attendee stands in the back of the room in order to escape at the first sign of boredom. The escape artist may even block the entrance.

The Painter

The painter uses a broad brush to categorize every speaker or activity. This attendee might say, "I sold a unit investment trust once and it lost money. I'm not interested in them anymore. I went out in a rowboat once and it turned over. I don't do cruises."

Lost

The lost person fails to read any preconference materials. Consequently, she doesn't know where to go, when the activities are, and when to be there. She says that she needs more information regarding activities at the conference because she spent too much time trying to figure out where to go.

The Sleeper

This attendee brazenly sleeps sitting up, often nodding off before a speaker begins. The usual complaint is of too many boring speakers.

The Talker

The talker often competes with the speaker. He always has a story about every comment a speaker makes and can't wait till the speaker finishes to tell it. Usually he keeps a whole table from listening to the speaker and still complains that there is not enough time for networking.

Shy

This attendee physically dodges a product sponsor or speaker, afraid she might try to sell him something. The usual complaint is that product sponsors are too close to sessions.

Once Is Enough

You might overhear a once-is-enough person saying: "Too many people are talking about the same thing. I have heard all of this before." This attendee doesn't know that repetition is good and that retention rate on first hearing is only 10 to 15 percent. She usually operates at 10 to 15 percent of her capability. She doesn't understand that we are all in the same business and that repetition is inevitable, that you can never hear the basics enough times. There are a thousand ways to tell the same story: Keep listening to the methods that really reach out and touch you.

The Penny-Pincher

The penny-pincher believes that the conference fees are too high and that all outside activities should be included in the fees. Frugality is good, but it must be combined with common sense. Fees paid for attending most broker-dealer conferences seldom cover the cost of meals and breaks. The remaining activities are provided to the participant free. A little polite attention is then expected.

What's the moral to these stories?

1. Mine for diamonds rather than for stones. There are always a few great ideas at even the worst conferences.
2. Remember that all of the mentioned types are well represented at every conference. The people putting on the conference can't possibly meet all of their needs. If they achieve a good balance, the conference is a success.
3. Review the conference materials before the conference. I know it is easier to wait until arrival to look at them, but it costs everyone more time in the long run.
4. Plan your activities in advance. Make a list of who you want to see, what questions you'd like to ask, and which

sessions you want to attend. Keep the list with you during the conference so that you can add to it as needed.

5. Carry a good ideas folder or small binder. Use big blank sheets of paper and write key words for tasks to complete when you return to the office.

6. Be on time for the sessions you wish to attend.

7. Never stand in the back of room and talk while a presentation is in session. To get the most benefit from any speaker, sit to her left and near the front.

8. Try to stay at the facility where the conference is being held. Even though there may be cheaper facilities nearby, you lose a lot of the spirit of the conference when you must come and go. Also, the organization putting on a conference in a hotel or resort has to make promises for a certain number of occupied rooms in order to get competitive rates.

9. Try to tune into the economics of the conference. Who is paying for what? If you paid a large fee to attend (i.e., if the attendee fees cover the cost of the conference) then you certainly can expect to see the people you want to see and engage in the activities you want to attend. However, if part or all of the cost of the conference is underwritten by others, then they also have a say in what goes on. Most broker-dealer conferences are largely underwritten by product sponsors who pay a fee to attend. They must be given the right to speak to the attendees in exchange for this underwriting. They should be treated as hosts, not unwelcome guests.

10. Recognize that financial planning is not a science. It is mostly common sense. If you enter this profession and attend conferences, continue your professional education, read, study, or engage in any type of learning, you are going to see a lot of repetition. Don't complain about it until you are good enough to say you know it all by heart and you have the results to prove it.

11. Be a good mentor and mentee. There will always be someone who can learn from you and someone whom you can learn from. Ask questions of the more successful partici-

pants. Offer your help to those who are less successful. Even if you are just starting, you can usually find someone else in the same boat. Get together and seek out a mentor.

TRADE ASSOCIATIONS AND OTHER GROUPS

I won't waste time and space by trying to list all of the organizations that financial consultants can join. Just as you can probably use credentials as a good reason for procrastination and not getting onto the real business of practicing financial planning for real people, you can probably overjoin. All of us have been to meetings where we see *professional attendees.* A typical day for these people might include reading the *Wall Street Journal* for the first two hours of the day, preparing for and attending luncheon meetings with their favorite professional groups until afternoon, then going to committee meetings of their favorite organizations in the afternoon. Professional attendees had better be on some sort of salary or be independently wealthy. You must allocate time to get down to the business of helping clients achieve their financial goals. That should be your focus.

That said, I also believe that you will find people at these associations who are at the top of their field. They are easy to find. They have found a way to balance their time for leadership in the profession with serving clients. You will probably want to lean more toward meeting with clients in the beginning so that you can build a solid client base. After the base is built, you will find that you have more time, as well as more expertise, to lend to associations.

That doesn't mean you should avoid associations and trade groups. You should join, but be selective in which ones you join and what time you can initially afford to devote to the organization. These organizations usually offer excellent opportunities not only for networking but also for learning and getting formal continuing professional education as well. The organizations also are active in legislative matters that affect the profession directly.

Which associations should you join? That will depend on many factors, such as your location, qualifications, and colleagues' chosen organizations. If you have mentors for this profession, ask their advice and perhaps follow in their footsteps. Many of the organizations have barriers to entry such as professional designations. If you qualify, you will be invited. If you don't, you need not apply.

The largest trade association for financial planning remains the International Association for Financial Planning. As indicated earlier, it had more than 24,000 members at one time, then shrank by more than half because of the limited partnership fiasco. It is now rebuilding and is up to more than 12,700 members. The IAFP is a trade association open to anyone who meets certain ethical requirements and is participating in the profession. I like the association because it includes mutual funds companies, all three groups of financial planners, companies who provide services to the industry, and broker-dealers. It offers excellent continuing professional education through its local chapters and its annual conference. The IAFP is consistently able to attract the leaders in the industry for speaking engagements. At the annual conference, you will see a cornucopia of products, services, and speakers. I highly recommend this association as your second real connection.

Other organizations that you will encounter as you become more experienced in financial planning include the Institute of Certified Financial Planners, the National Association of Personal Financial Advisors (a fee-only group), and the American Society of CLU/ChFC. Each of the professional credentials (including CFP, CFA, and ChFC) usually has its own national organization. Many have local chapters.

One of the companies you should be familiar with is the Investment Company Institute. It is made up of more than 400 investment companies (mutual funds companies). It represents the industry in Washington and provides educational material for financial consultants and the general public to increase awareness of financial planning. The institute can be reached at P.O. Box 27850, Washington, D.C. 20038-7850.

MAGAZINES AND BOOKS

There are hundreds of books that could be read about various aspects of financial planning. I have written a couple myself, including *The CPA's Guide to a Successful Financial Planning Practice* and *Financial Planning: The CPA's Practice Guide*. If I gave you a complete list of books to read, most people would be overwhelmed and wouldn't read any of them. Don't worry about reading a huge number of books at first. Remember to take things one step at a time. Our company offers a suggested reading list of books, tapes, and periodicals. I have heard that reading one hour a day in your chosen profession will make you qualified in your field in only one year. Reading one hour per day for two years will make you one of the best in the profession and ahead of most of your peer group. In only five years, you can become a leading authority. I believe this to be true. Thoreau said "How many a man has dated an era in his life from the reading of a book?"

It is a cliché to say that experience is the best teacher. I believe that experience gained concurrently with reading increases your comprehension at least tenfold. You will see the need for specific knowledge in your field as you design your success plan and begin working with clients. If you decide to go after a professional designation, new books will be introduced. Most of the professional associations and trade organizations have their own magazines. I highly recommend magazines for getting you connected fast. Sometimes more accessible than books, magazines can keep you abreast of what is happening in the industry and what your peer groups are doing. I subscribe to about 15 industry magazines and newsletters. Here are the names of a few to get you started:

Financial Planning. This is the official magazine of the IAFP. You can subscribe at 40 West 57th Street, New York, New York 10019.

Dow Jones Investment Advisor. 179 Avenue at the Common, Shrewsbury, New Jersey 07702.

Registered Representative. Information about subscribing can be obtained by writing Plaza Communications, 18818 Teller Avenue, Suite 280, Irvine, California 92715.

As an outsider looking in, it may seem very difficult to become involved in the profession. Expect that to get tougher as time goes by. Many on the inside now want the barriers raised.

Numerous consumer groups and legislators want more regulation. Getting connected today is relatively easy. Just become a registered representative, take advantage of the network already in place with your broker-dealer, then join the IAFP. The professional organizations and credentials will start to come into focus when you are ready.

7

BUILDING A SOLID
FINANCIAL PLANNING
PRACTICE

Building a successful financial planning practice involves the familiar catch 22 of needing experience to get a job but not being able to get a job without experience. You need clients to get experience but can't get clients without experience. It is not easy to overcome this barrier, but people do it everyday and you can, too. In this chapter, I will offer strategies that have been thoroughly tested and proven successful on how to build a solid base of clients. I do not have a secret formula, however. You will have to exert some effort and take some risk. You have to want to be a successful financial planner enough to pay the price.

There are lots of ways to enter the profession. You can start working for someone else in the financial planning business in order to gain experience. Working for a wirehouse will offer the opportunity for training in products, selling, and working with clients. You could go to work for a broker-dealer in training, back-office, or marketing areas of the firm. You might take a job working for an investment company to learn how the system works. In all these situations, you are gaining experience, but you are not building a clientele that belongs to you.

In order to start building your own business, you might look for an experienced financial consultant who needs a partner or potential future owner. Or you could start your own firm from scratch. Both are viable solutions, but each involves different risks. Some are easier in the beginning and tougher in the end, and others reverse that process. Many aspiring financial consultants will decide in advance which avenue they want to follow and design a plan of action around that goal. Others will consider their individual circumstances and let those guide their decisions. For example, they may have a referral or influence with an existing financial planning firm that will lead to their joining that firm. They may have relatives in the business that need future buyers. Most, however, will have to make the decision without any definite arrows pointing toward one path or another. My advice is to not let your comfort zone be your primary guide. The comfort zone can be the worst place to make decisions. You should wind up doing what you like to do, but you may have to suffer some discomfort and risk to get where you want to go. Think long term when making your initial foray into the business. If you have a good idea of where you want to be in five, ten, or twenty years, then that should guide your decision.

SETTING GOALS

Sitting down at your computer or with a simple pad and pencil to *think* and *visualize* about where you want to be in the future is the most important step in entering any career or profession. That advice also applies to your personal life, but I will confine my remarks here to your professional life. You must decide how successful you want to be and you must decide in advance. That's a problem for many people. How can you know how successful you want to be? In terms of money, I will give you some guidelines in chapter 8. You can set goals in terms of number of clients, assets under management, number of client contacts made in a day, or annual, monthly, weekly, or daily income. Others may resist talking about money and want to concentrate on services rendered to clients. Either is acceptable. However, if you have a problem with talking about making a lot of money, then you may be unnecessarily positioning yourself with a low-income mentality. *Making money for yourself and your family should not be in conflict with helping clients in financial planning.*

It is difficult to write about the necessity of putting the client first and not making decisions based on commissions, while simultaneously saying that it is all right to set goals for your own income. I know that causes confusion for some. However, these are not conflicting goals; in fact, you can bring them into perfect harmony. You will learn that the more you put your clients' welfare ahead of your own, the more you will prosper. That is a wonderful discovery. Of course, wise people have known this for centuries. It just took me longer to catch on.

Still having trouble visualizing yourself five or ten years from now? Having more trouble putting numbers on your income levels? Don't worry. This is not etched in stone. Allow yourself some quiet time to think about your goals, visualize and dream, and write down what results. For this process to work best, the goals will be adjusted as you get more comfortable with them and with yourself in your new career.

MARKETING

I have assumed that most readers will eventually want to build a quality, successful financial planning practice. If you have zero clients and nothing but a set of goals, where do you start? You start with a plan for success. I used to hate to hear that from a writer or speaker. Most plans I had been associated with were lots of canned words, spreadsheets full of numbers, and a few charts and graphs. Then I learned that a success plan involved much more than a spreadsheet with projections. It should be your dream sheet, your ticket to paradise, or whatever personal name you like. The plan should come to life in your mind and be framed as a major point of reference in your quest for success.

Your goals are the first step in that plan. You can now take your goals and turn them into specific action steps in various categories, put target dates on each step, and then start working the plan. Working the plan will involve marketing and selling. What's the difference? I think of marketing as finding clients to sell to and selling as getting them to buy from you or take the actions you recommend. However, it is often impossible to separate them since many major marketing steps involve the selling process. My goal in this chapter is to make you comfortable with both. As I said in the beginning, I do not have a magic formula that pours money into your account without much effort. However, I do have a success formula that works. It just takes courage, determination, and persistence to make it work.

Designing Your Success Plan

Before you take off on a binge of cold calling, direct mail campaigns, or seminars, you need a plan. The recipe for building a solid financial planning practice requires a mixture of good planning with a large quantity of *action.* Shy planners are too heavy on planning and fail to recognize that they must eventually *implement* their plans. Planners who love people interaction and have good skills may go off in several directions at once and never learn why they are not more successful. I think most people have a natural inclination to do the thing they are most comfortable with; that often leads to procrastination or activity without a direction in other areas. Try these steps toward building your plan for success.

Set up five folders or small ring binders with these titles:

1. Client list
2. Success plan target clients
3. Success plan target services and products
4. Success plan ideas to implement
5. Success plan tools

Keep these folders in plain sight in your work area. As ideas come to you, write them on an 8½" by 11" sheet of paper and place them in the appropriate folders.

Client List

In folder number one start listing the potential clients for your services. If you have a few clients already, list them first. If you have customers, clients, or fellow employees in your current profession, list them second. Now list all of the people from whom you purchase goods and services. Fourth, list your friends and other acquaintances who might be in need of financial planning. Fifth, list the types of businesses that you like or have experience in. For example, if you are leaving a defense plant job to go into financial planning, you might want to become an expert in financial planning for people in that particular industry. If your family ran a retail clothing store, then you might want to start specializing in that type of client. If you or a family member or close acquaintance is a dentist or member of a similar profession, consider medical financial planning as a possible specialty. If your hobby is sailing, consider the people who sail, their clubs, where they get their boats and accessories, and so forth. Finally, list family members who would be easy to work with and are possibly in need of financial planning assistance.

Don't expect these lists to just roll off your brain at once. They will come to you at various times. Just don't forget to write them down. Don't worry about any particular order or priority or even about keeping separate lists, just write them down. You can categorize and prioritize later. If you are like most people, these lists will give you a lot more confidence: You already have a client list!

Target Clients

In folder number 2, place ideas about whom you want to market to and the products or services that might interest them. This is a two-pronged thought process of *who* and *what*. Who do you want to market to? What products or services do you want to market? Let's examine the *who* question first. Which people constitute your preferred market? I can't give you an answer, but I will give you some sample questions so that you can reach your own conclusions.

1. Which group do you think you would prefer working with—the affluent or the average?
2. Do you prefer working with the very young or older adults? Professional or blue collar?

3. Do you want a large and diverse client base in which client contact is limited by necessity or a close-knit client base where service is very personal and client contact frequent?

4. What is your own background? With whom do you feel most comfortable having social and business contacts?

I don't feel that the decision about your eventual client base has to be made up front, but it helps if you can get some general guidance as to whom you prefer working with. Many financial planners should start working with clients at all income levels to get training. Personal experiences gained from working with the various groups will guide them as to the future direction of their practice.

Target Services and Products

The second part of target marketing is to compile a list of products and services that your preferred market would be likely to need and appreciate. Write these ideas down and place them in folder number 3. Here are some examples from my own marketing plan that you can begin with. Remember, however, that this list should largely be your own, not mine. Throw out the market segments that you aren't interested in and add others. You must *own* this list. That is, it must come from your own creative thought processes. Which of your clients might be interested in the following?

> *Retirement plans:* 401Ks, 403 Bs, 457s, profit sharing, nonqualified, SEP, and SAR-SEPs.
>
> *Retirement planning:* May include investing lump-sum distributions and dealing with the tax consequences and selecting retirement locations, avocations, and vocations.
>
> *Business continuation planning:* For owners of businesses. How do they plan for the orderly transfer and continuance of the business to new owners or heirs in the event of disability, retirement, or death?
>
> *Payroll deduction and cafeteria plans*
>
> *Traditional insurance:* Life, disability, health, long-term care, and so forth.
>
> *Estate planning*

Insurance as an investment: Annuities, variable life

Financial planning and taxes

Financial planning as an employee benefit: Offering workshops for employees of businesses.

Education funding

Planning for the Elderly

Industry or profession specialization: Planning for the medical profession is enjoying growth now because of the changes in the medical profession caused by HMOs and other health provider groups.

Product specialization: You may have an affinity for stock selection, annuities, mutual funds, and tax-exempt securities.

This is not a complete list. Add to it as you come across specialty areas in the profession that have special interest to you.

Ideas

Now we are ready for folder number 4. In this folder, drop all the ideas about action steps you can take that have occurred to you about the first three folders. Don't worry, you won't draw a blank. If you have started the thought process by using the first three folders, ideas have already come into your head. Write each idea on the same size paper and drop it into this folder as it occurs to you. A lot of your ideas will come to you when you are just going to sleep, in a dream, or when you are away from the office. Don't ignore them. Write them down as they occur to you and drop them in the folder later.

Tools

Folder number 5 includes the tools that you may use to develop and implement your success plan. I call this folder a reference or reminder folder. I look in this folder when I am trying to reach a certain client or type of client. The list refreshes my memory of the various things I might use or do to reach that client or group. I look inside it for inspiration when I am writing down my action ideas for each part of my success plan. Include in this folder all the tangible *things* as well as the intangible *methods* of making your plan successful. Examples of items to be included in this folder include the following:

Seminars

Direct mail

Financial plans

Tax returns

Prospectuses and annual reports from mutual funds or other products

Marketing material from product sponsors

Portfolio monitor reports for clients

Press releases

Radio or TV shows

Articles for the press

Advertising

Newsletters

Public speaking scripts

Materials from clubs, associations, and so forth

Brochures, business cards, and stationery

Referrals

We now have five folders with client lists, target clients, target services and products, ideas, and methods and tools. If your five folders are not coming together in your mind or taking physical forms on the written page, try going to your favorite place of seclusion and devoting a day or two to just thinking about your plan. I know you don't believe you have time to think, but you really can't afford not to take the time. Just reframe your point of reference and look at thinking as the most productive use of your time.

Now let's pull it all together.

1. Set up a page for each target service or product (e.g., 403B retirement plans).
2. Write down the targeted clients you think will be most interested in this service or product (e.g., teachers, employees of hospitals).

3. Write down your goal(s) for this target market segment (e.g., develop 25 clients who contribute to 403Bs by 12/31/97).

4. List all the ideas from folder four that apply to this target market as action steps to be taken to reach your goal. If you have none or only one, go to folder five to spur your thought process. Each idea might be its own action step or it may be a project that requires you to list action steps that must be taken to make the idea work.

5. Assign target dates for each idea and project or action step/task and delegate responsibility for some tasks to staff, if possible.

6. Assign tasks in your time-management system for each idea or action step.

7. Start doing the steps in priority order. Some can be done during the same day or week, others require complete focus or must be done sequentially. These distinctions will be obvious when the plan is done. Some can be assigned to lower-level staff members, others you will have to do yourself. Of course, this is one of the main reasons for having a plan to start with.

The success plan you design will bring focus, clarity, and efficiency to your efforts. It should be reviewed at least monthly for needed changes. You should have an automated time-management system that reminds you of the tasks. From this point on, it is simply a matter of taking action. You must perform the tasks or take them off the market plan. Your focused, directed activity will yield results.

SELLING

If the word strikes fear or even disgust in your mind or heart, get over it. I don't know of any successful careers that don't involve selling in some fashion. Certainly some of it is easier than others, but most people have to sell either themselves or a product. In financial planning, you are generally selling yourself. However, you will also have to convince your clients to take action that they may *need* to take, but don't *have* to take. You will also have to sell around your competitors, the client's friends, other advisors, and financial gurus of all ilks.

Many people say that selling is a numbers game. If you ask enough people to buy, a certain number will eventually say yes. You have to get a certain number of negative answers before you get a yes. That means that hearing no is a positive process on the way to getting yeses. Many salespeople start each day with an attitude of accumulating nos so that they can get them out of the way before the yeses start rolling in. I like and admire the people who can stand that type of punishment, but I don't believe that most people can. You certainly have to develop enough self-confidence to keep a rejection or two from devastating you, but you don't have to take continuous, daily rejection. That is what a success plan is for.

To approach selling in a positive manner, I learned the process I referred to earlier as *reframing*. I started looking at things from a different perspective. Instead of thinking of selling financial plans, products, or even my services, I think of myself as the provider of solutions to clients' financial problems. Almost everyone has a financial planning problem of some sort. I will identify those problems and develop a suitable solution. If I am asked what I do for a living, I respond accordingly: I help people remove obstacles to their financial goals or assist them in designing financial road maps leading to their financial goals.

How does this view work in real-world client situations? I went to many sales seminars and tried various techniques to get clients to take the actions I felt they should. When the techniques did not work for me, I tried reframing my point of reference again. I learned to develop what I call *empathy, sympathy,* and *caring* feelings for my clients. I empathized with their feelings by sharing my own similar struggles. I felt genuine sympathy for their financial struggles and expressed that sympathy sincerely. I shared other experiences so that the clients did not feel they were alone with their problems. I cared about the problems in my clients' lives. Does that mean I did not care before I started providing financial planning services? While I cared, I did not allow these feelings to come to the surface or to enter my mind with their full force lest they take away my professionalism or, worse, take up billable time. I learned to spend a lot more time *listening* and a lot less time talking. I also learned how to ask easy, nonthreatening questions. How did I learn how to do all of these things? *I practiced!* Clients know when you care about them. They can sense it. It is true that they are much more concerned with how much you care than how much you know.

TOPS

How did I practice and get good at my client relationships? I developed my own formula to follow in sales situations. I learned what top-producing sales executives do. They don't beat their heads against the wall every day, accumulating nos even though rejection doesn't generally bother them. They put every effort into making every presentation successful. I have already shared that preparing financial plans will enhance your chance of success. However, even when I am working with a client and a financial plan is not involved, I will use this formula. The acronym for my formula is *TOPS*. Each letter signifies a stage in the sales process and the type of question that must be asked in the various stages. That doesn't mean that all clients will allow you to go in sequential order. The fact that clients skip around is one of the primary reasons for the formula. It keeps the planner focused on what stage of the sales process they are in.

> *T stands for trust.* In this stage, you are establishing or reaffirming trust with the client. Trust questions might simply be about the length of the relationship between the planner and the client, or they might be about mutual interests or common relationships. Don't spend all day establishing trust. Some is there already, or the client would not be meeting with you.
>
> *O stands for opportunity.* These questions refer to the client's problem(s). If you are discussing a financial plan, these questions might simply be a restatement of the stated goals or objectives on the client's financial plan. If you are working from other data, these questions would zero in on problems that the client needs to solve. A typical opportunity question is "How do you plan on paying for your children's education?"

P stands for pain. I also say that it stands for personalization of the problem. This is key to the sales process. Most clients will not really see the severity of the problem from the questions about opportunity. They will simply see it as your problem as a financial planner or a feeble attempt to sell them something. A pain question helps the client to see the consequences of not solving the problem. It makes the client uncomfortable to *not* solve the problem. As a follow-up to the opportunity question, the consultant might say "What are you going to tell young Robert Jr. in 2011 when he is ready to start college at SMU? Did you know that the first semester may cost up to $12,000? That his first degree could cost well over $100,000 by that time?" With these questions, you have created a visual image for the client of her son asking for $12,000 and a desperate parent looking around for the money.

S stands for solution. After clients are made aware of the consequences of not solving the problem, they are usually ready for the solution. Simply present a solution to the problem, indicate that you are prepared to implement it, and shut up. The solution to a college funding problem will usually be as simple as putting aside a set amount each month until the child reaches college age. I seldom mention products except in generic terms until clients are prepared to implement solutions. Mentioning products gives clients the opportunity to escape the problem and talk about performance. Performance gives them an excuse for not doing something about the problem. After clients have agreed to solve the problem, go over products in the implementation stage.

When using TOPS, remember to *listen* to clients' responses to your questions. Notice what parts of the sales process the clients are in. If you are offering a solution while the clients are developing trust, you need to get back to that point. Finally, *relax.* Don't push the sale. Adopt the perspective of knowing that you have done your best to solve the problem. If clients don't take action, it's their own fault. You have done your best. If they don't follow your advice now, maybe they will do so later. I know that it is easier said than done, but when you finally relax, your income will increase dramatically because clients will sense the release of tension.

OTHER MARKETING AND CLIENT SERVICE IDEAS

Here are some other ideas I have used successfully:

- From the local paper, newsletters, and so forth, cut out items of interest about clients and send them copies with notes of congratulations.
- Join community service organizations. Volunteer work will lead to positions of leadership and influence. Don't just do it for the increased business, however. Adopt an altruistic attitude. The key word, again, is balance. You can overvolunteer. Don't volunteer to avoid working in your practice.
- Adopt a system for reporting to clients on the status of their plans. A report on investment performance may be the central focus, but don't limit your report to investment status; also report on progress toward goals. Make the clients feel good about doing something.
- Send thank you notes for referrals and when clients implement any of your suggestions. This gives clients a feeling of affirmation at just the time when they may be experiencing postpurchase remorse.
- Keep in touch. Call for nonbusiness reasons just to say hello to clients. If you try to make a sale every time you call, clients will be suspicious.
- Do things for clients for no compensation. Help them with a problem not related to financial matters and don't send a bill.
- Always clearly define expectations, then exceed them.
- Call clients by their names and know their habits. Keep index cards on how they like their coffee, nicknames, and so forth. Let your staff know about the importance of calling clients by their names.
- Host appreciation events for your clients. This could be a dinner party or casual drinks and snacks.

- Get testimonial letters from clients.
- Make house calls. Don't be rigid as to meeting location.
- Consider the special needs of older adults. Speak slowly and use big print. Design everything so that a 60-year-old can read it. Thirty-somethings usually can read either big *or* small print.
- Keep the information simple. Remember the KISS principle: Keep It Short and Simple.
- Contact centers of influence. This could be CPAs, attorneys, or other advisors who do not do financial planning but advise clients in related areas and who hold positions of influence and trust with people you want for clients.
- Don't let money drop through the cracks. Many planners will spend hours designing a plan of action for a client. The client will implement about half the plan, procrastinating or promising to implement the other half later. Instead of following up with this client, the planner will spend time trying to find new clients and designing new plans. The best treasures are found in your own backyard. Finish implementing plans for existing clients. After all, most of the work is already done.
- Ask for referrals. Businesses are built on the three Rs: Responsiveness to existing clients, referrals, and retention. All three Rs are indispensable in building a solid practice.

TIPS FOR RUNNING YOUR OWN BUSINESS

Keep the Books

Don't be the bare-footed cobbler. You are running a business, and you have to pay attention to it. Run it as you would advise your clients to run theirs. You must know the basics of accounting and taxation. With today's technology, there is simply no excuse for not having monthly financial statements to track your progress toward your goals. You must spend time analyzing whether marketing and other expenses were good investments. The key here is to have balance. Don't get paralysis by analysis. Just because a marketing expense didn't result in immediate revenues doesn't make it a bad expense.

Don't Get Hung Up on Rates per Hour

If you keep comparing what you earn in the first year or two to what you could make in salary with a large corporation with a nice benefits package, you are not an entrepreneur. Remember the energy reward formula and think long term. Big expenditures of energy equal small rewards in the short term. Bigger rewards come from less effort in the long term. How much do you want to work for yourself?

Select the Right Form of Business

I know they taught this process in beginning business courses, but you need to think about it. I recommend not making hasty decisions. Operate as a sole proprietorship until you clearly see the need for a corporation. Even then, I would think twice. I prefer sole proprietorships. If you have a partner, then plan on a partnership or a corporation. Limited liability companies offer some benefits of a corporation, sole proprietorship, and partnerships.

Select a Good Location

You can be successful operating from your home if you have a big need to keep overhead to a minimum, but I recommend a tasteful office with easy access as soon as possible.

Don't Buy More Software Than You Need

It's probably still true about buying software first, then buying hardware to match, but hardware is pretty well defined in the PC market today. Certain items are essential. The market changes daily, but it's still best to buy state-of-the-art equipment, especially for limited space requirements. It doesn't cost that much more and can save you a lot of grief. As for financial planning software, I wouldn't buy any until I could do a financial plan without it. A lot of good software is free or close to it when you work through product sponsors.

Take a Time-Management Course

Most people are very poor time managers. Buy yourself a couple of books on the subject or take a course if you keep wondering where the time goes.

AVOIDING THE TEN MOST COMMON MISTAKES

I made a lot of mistakes when I entered the profession. In training financial planners today, I find that most make the same ones that I did. The mistakes are repeated regularly enough to be predictable. Most planners new to the profession will commit seven of these ten mistakes.

Mistake #1   Failing to Take Your Own Medicine

Many financial planners spend years in the profession making recommendations to clients that they don't follow themselves. As a result, their own financial houses are not in order. They don't have their own plans. Clients sense this lack of belief in planners' recommendations for them.

Mistake #2   Elephant Hunting with an Unloaded Gun While Ignoring Pet Rabbits That Will Eat Out of Your Hand

For reasons I don't understand, most new financial consultants start going after the biggest, most complex schemes or clients right out of the gate. I call this elephant hunting with an unloaded gun because they are going after big clients with complex problems or big administrative headaches that the beginning planner is ill equipped to handle. Also, they usually will have to compete with more experienced planners with deeper resources. Instead, go after the pet rabbits, clients who trust you already and have problems that are easy to identify and solve. My only explanation for this tendency of new planners is fear of failure and the desire to "save" the easy clients. If they go after a big deal, they are not expected to get it. The result is less sense of failure. If they go after a pet rabbit and fail, then they may consider giving up before they get a good start. Avoid this tendency. If the first few pet rabbits don't act, the next one will.

Mistake #3   Procrastinating

Most beginning planners will do anything to avoid dealing with the real heart of planning: meeting with a client and doing a financial plan for that client. They want to get a Ph.D. in swimming before they get in the water. Beginners will analyze software, read the magazines, read the *Wall Street Journal,* or do anything to avoid possible rejection. You can and must do all these things *while* you are working with clients. Your learning experience value will multiply exponentially if you are learning at the same time you are helping clients.

Mistake #4   Putting Product Selection First

Planners often see their primary value as product pickers. This leads them to start talking to clients about yield and performance and this leads to client disappointments. Although products must be discussed, they should almost never be the basis for clients making a decision to follow your recommendations. After they have decided to take steps you recommend, products can be explained. Past performance, in the proper context as no guarantee or indicator of future performance, may also be discussed if clients wish.

Mistake #5   Insisting on Doing Everything Yourself

I agree that overhead must be kept low for a beginning planner, but when you add staff, give them responsibility and allow them to be trained along with you. There is a lot to be said for bringing on an assistant at the start, even with the increased overhead. I prefer hiring a good assistant rather than a receptionist or file clerk. A good assistant will assist in handling mundane office duties, as well as problem solving and more complex duties as training is made available. If you want to build a large practice, extra assistance is going to be essential.

Mistake #6   Playing Hide-and-Seek

Lots of planners use the avoidance technique of hiding behind prospectuses, mailers, videos, brochures, and software. Although this is just another procrastination technique, it is repeated enough to have its own mistake number. These consultants do what is easy and quick with very little risk of rejection. They never speak directly to clients about financial planning. They let the videos, brochures, and prospectuses do it for them. Clients will not buy from strangers on a video. These are tools, not substitutes for you. A planner who plays hide-and-seek has not done a success plan and is just working without positive direction.

Mistake #7   Never Trying On a Client's Shoes

These planners see only textbook solutions. They don't learn to get inside clients' heads and hearts. They fail to learn and practice empathy, sympathy, and caring. Clients know this instinctively and never let such planners get past their trust questions in the TOPS formula. Think how you like to be treated when you are paying for advice and consultation on anything, then treat your clients that way.

Mistake #8   Hiding from Clients when Investments Go South

Invariably, markets will correct and performance will be negative or disappointing. Good planners will race to the phone, fax, or computer to discuss this situation with their clients. That is what planners get paid to do. When clients hear nothing, they expect the worst.

Mistake #9   Confusing Technical Jargon with Good Communication

Some planners want to impress clients with how much they know when clients only want to know how much planners care. Clients will usually readily accept that you are technically competent, but not necessarily that you have their best interests at heart. That is one of the reasons I always stress repetitive training. Good planners should know their stuff so well that they can teach it to others. That takes repetition. Many planners will not attend the same training session twice. Be aware of the rule of nine: It takes nine repetitions before you completely absorb all of the information in a session that is longer than two hours. I don't mean to imply that you must attend nine sessions before you are competent, just don't balk at repetition. You can never hear the basics in this business too often. Someone once said that true genius is the ability to reduce the complicated to the simple. Do you like for someone to talk over *your* head?

Mistake #10   Failing to Take Responsibility

This is probably the most common cause of failure in most endeavors: blaming conditions, markets, clients, family, broker-dealers, and regulators for all the problems encountered. Certainly all of these groups can place obstacles in your path to success; often, you cannot control those obstacles. You can, however, control how you react to the obstacles. You must concentrate more on finding a way to get around them, remove them, or overcome them and less on complaining about them.

SEQUENTIAL STEPS TO SUCCESS

I have covered a lot of information about entering this profession in a book that is not intended to be in-depth about financial planning. You may be overwhelmed. Many of the people I train in courses are confused as to which of the many required steps to take first. The result is usually failure to take any steps. I don't have a formula for success that applies to everyone, but I offer my suggestions for sequential action steps here. You can change them around as your needs dictate.

1. Select a broker-dealer and get licensed as a registered representative. This may not be the major source of your future income, but it connects to a great training network. It is hard to make a mistake by taking this step. Make sure training is a priority with your broker-dealer. Take the test to become a registered representative and the insurance exam to allow you to sell annuities and traditional insurance. See Appendix B for information about the licensing process.

2. Connect to all the training you can get through your new broker-dealer sponsor network. Get as smart as you can as cheaply as you can this way.

3. Select a core group of products based on the information shared in chapter 4. Study your core group and visit with their wholesalers and home office.

4. Gather your own data and prepare a financial plan for yourself. Your broker-dealer should be able to provide you with forms or software. Forms are preferable, so that your work will be a creative endeavor, not canned software.

5. Using your own products, implement the easiest of your recommended solutions for your own financial problems.

6. Create your success plan using the steps outlined in this chapter.

7. Implement the easiest and most obvious action steps in your success plan.

8. Select "pet rabbits" from your client list and offer to do free financial plans for them. Again, focus on the problems that are easiest to solve.

9. Subscribe to the best magazines and periodicals in the field. Keep getting connected to the profession. See chapter 6.

10. Enter another formal training program (possibly the CFP or another of your choice). See details in chapters 5 and 6.

11. Implement any remaining steps in your own financial plan and keep it updated.

12. Repeat step 8 over and over.
13. Keep building your network in accordance with your success plan.
14. Train, train, and retrain at every opportunity. Repetition is good.
15. Keep working on your success plan.

8

HOW FINANCIAL PLANNERS GET PAID

Much is written in the financial press and for the general public about how financial planners get paid. It has been a subject of controversy since the beginning of the profession. Just as we are continually trying to define what we will call ourselves, we also struggle with how we will be fairly compensated. The media seldom mention that the way consumers pay for financial services must make economic sense for both the *provider* and the *receiver* of the services. Discussing that financial consultants must make a living may not be politically correct, but my experience is that clients don't expect you to work for free. In fact, they want you to be successful. Who wants a broke financial planner? Clients just want to know how you are paid and that they are getting the best deal for their money.

My clients also like to be informed about their choices of payment. They appreciate frank discussions about what is economically feasible for both the client and the financial planner. That way, they can make informed decisions. Planners must also be able to make choices if they are not going to limit their practices to a certain clientele. It is not economically feasible to charge by the hour for some clients. Time-based and asset-based fees and commissions are also only appropriate for some clients. Clients just want the best deal they can get with their particular circumstances. They don't want to find out after the fact that they made a bad choice. After informing clients about choices, planners should discuss how they would *like* to get paid by the clients and why. If consultants limit their practices to only one method of payment, they should also recognize that their client base is going to be limited to clients who are appropriate for that method of compensation. When there is not a fit, clients should be informed of the situation and referred elsewhere.

Most clients who use financial planners today are not well informed about payment methods. Of course, the majority of the population that has never used financial planners has little but negative information about their compensation. Who is to blame for this mess? The media must take part of the blame. Their reporting takes the path of least resistance, and the easiest thing to do is to find fault with anyone's method of compensation. It is easy to put on the cape of the great protector of consumers; ferreting out the negatives is easy and sells more magazines and newspapers. It is much more difficult to report about how people get paid and the *value* that planners bring to most people.

The financial planning profession and the industry as a whole must also take a large share of the blame. We have left ourselves vulnerable to criticism, with a cloak and dagger approach to compensation. We have been sometimes guilty of putting commissions before clients' best interests. We have churned (frequent trading with no real economic purpose or client benefit) clients' accounts to generate commissions. We have sold products that had dubious tax advantages and high commissions, but little economic benefit. Today the profession is engaged in internal struggles about which methods of compensation are good and which are evil. Many groups have taken the ivory tower approach that our way is the only way. This attitude not only keeps much of the public confused, it excludes them from badly needed financial products and advice. Mutual funds and insurance companies have used deceptive practices to mask commissions. Even consumers have been guilty of failing to do their homework and demanding get-rich-quick schemes. Of course, we cannot ask the consumer to take any of the blame. If we assist a client in doing the wrong thing and we know it is wrong, we must take full responsibility.

METHODS OF COMPENSATION

Salary

According to the 1995 NEFE survey mentioned earlier, approximately 7 percent of certified financial planners are paid strictly salary and another 6 percent received a combination of salary and commission. In the 1988 survey, no CFPs were paid strictly salary. The question about salary and commissions wasn't asked, which indicates a change in the profession. I think it suggests that many financial planning firms have grown large enough to hire salaried staffs, and that bodes especially well for the beginning financial planner. A salaried position with a quality financial planning firm is an excellent way to learn the business. Many CFPs also work for broker-dealers, investment companies, insurance companies, CPA firms, other investment product sponsors, and industry in general. The CFP is often sought by individuals for personal improvement and to learn how to plan their own financial lives. Many people currently working in industry also hold the CFP as a safety net for possible job loss or as a second career option.

Commissions

Commissions come from many sources and are earned and paid in a variety of ways. Most commissions come from sales of mutual funds, individual securities, annuities, and traditional insurance products.

Mutual Funds

Mutual funds now have their own alphabet soup of types of commissions. Only a few years ago, there were one or two ways to get paid. The vast majority of funds worked on up-front commissions, meaning the commission was taken from clients' funds the day the transaction was completed. If the gross commission was 4 percent on a $100,000 purchase in a mutual fund, then clients would see their investments drop to $96,000 instantly. For purposes of this initial discussion, I am ignoring break points that may reduce a gross commission. These will be discussed later. Up-front commissions could go as high as 8.5 percent when I entered the business. I don't know of any commissions that high today; the average is around 3.5 to 4.0 percent. Formerly, financial planners had little or no flexibility as to what commission the clients paid. Planners received a portion of this gross commission based on the payout rate they had with their broker-dealers (more on payout schedules later and in chapter 6). Payout rates range from about 25 to 95 percent.

Suppose that financial planners have $100,000 of the clients' money to invest. If the financial advisers were simply presenting or selling a product and not doing a financial plan, then they could easily get through their presentations and the paperwork in less than an hour for this $100,000 investment. If the commission is 4 percent and their payout rate 80 percent then they could make $3,200 in that hour. If you consider that they only worked an hour, then that's pretty good pay. Most clients will balk at that rate. However, if consultants actually prepare a plan and continue to work with the clients and report to them about their investments over regular periods for as long as the investment is under their guidance, then the $3,200 can look pretty small after five or six years of monthly or quarterly reports and meetings and lots of phone calls. The obvious question is whether the consultants will truly earn that $3,200 over the long-term relationship by spending time with the clients and monitoring their investments. True planners will earn the money, others will earn the rest of us a bad reputation by simply going onto another transaction and leaving clients to fend for themselves.

Can the clients earn the $3,200 back through superior financial planning (not just selection of products) as a result of assistance from planners? To earn their fees in terms of real dollars, financial consultants must improve the clients' long-term rates of return enough to make up the 4 percent commission that the clients paid up front. Can good financial planners do that? I believe that they can do that and more for most clients, because the clients are usually sporadic savers rather than investors before they engage the services of a financial consultant. Also, it is not entirely fair to judge the consultants' worth on whether they can earn back the commission through superior investment performance. As I related in the previous chapter, planners offer much more value than superior investment performance; however, they are often judged by this factor alone. You can see why there is controversy over commissions.

ABCD and other shares refer to the various types of shares that can be purchased from most mutual fund families. A lot of literature attempts to prove the benefits of one share type over another, but I don't think this is possible. All conditions would have to be the same regarding the date of purchase, time held, date of sale, and so forth. You can create a set of numbers to prove or disprove either theory, but the numbers will not work when the market or the client does something different than your assumptions. In general, A shares may be the cheapest way to pay commissions if the clients are long-term investors (minimum of five years). The longer they hold the shares, the better A shares look. However, I don't think this should be the only basis for advising clients about which type to buy. The decision should also focus on what makes the clients and their advisors comfortable. If the clients would rather not have their commissions deducted all at once, then they should be introduced to B or C shares.

> *A shares* are the traditional front-load types. The commission is deducted from the clients' investments as soon as they are made.
>
> *B shares* usually pay the same commission to the planners as A shares, but the commission is not deducted from the clients' investment. With this type of share, the clients see their entire investment go to work at once. They sound better on the surface, but B shares carry a contingent deferred sales charge. If clients withdraw their investments before a specified period, they will be hit with a sales charge (read: commission). This surrender charge, penalty for premature withdrawal, or contingent deferred sales charge (CDSC) usually starts at 5 percent and declines by 1 percent per year until it disappears. Since the mutual fund is paying the representative a commission up front, it has to finance that

"loan." This situation results in slightly higher expenses for B shares than for A shares.

C shares vary slightly from mutual fund to mutual fund. However, they usually share some similar characteristics. I call C shares a level load–type share. Clients normally do not pay any commission up front. The shares may have a small surrender charge if surrendered within one year. They generally pay commissions to the representatives quarterly for as long as clients remain invested. This commission is usually 1 percent per year paid in quarterly increments.

D shares pay an annual asset-based fee to representatives similar to C shares but also may charge a small up-front commission.

Y shares are usually sold to institutional investors. They are purchased by money managers and institutions without a sales charge.

Z shares are for employees of mutual funds companies.

POP, MOP, and NAV refer to the pricing of shares for distribution. POP stands for public offering price, the price that the investor pays for shares, including the sales charge. It is higher, of course, than the real market value of the share because it includes commissions. MOP is a term I have seen only recently to describe the same thing, calling it market offering price. NAV refers to net asset value, the true market value of the share. NAV is determined by pricing all the holdings in the fund each day at market value and dividing by the number of shares. Why complicate things so much with these terms?

I don't really know the history of POP and NAV, but I can make a good guess as to the reason for their existence. In the early days of mutual funds, most if not all commissions were paid up front. Many were higher than the 8.5 percent they were when I entered the business. If clients invested $100,000 with a representative and immediately saw it drop to $91,500 or less on their first statements, it could be quite a shock. We all know that it shouldn't have been a shock, because the representative should have explained it earlier in the process. Of course, many didn't. To cushion this shock, a POP price per share was calculated. This way customers could multiply the number of shares they bought by the POP and arrive at their total investment. Not until the next statement did they see the NAV price. Most customers attributed this decrease to a market drop, or simply failed to make the calculation again until several months later. Hopefully, by the time the customers saw that a commission had been deducted from their statements, dividends and increases in the price per share had at least partially made up for the commissions paid.

To some, my analysis may seem cynical or harsh. To others, it may look like the mutual funds took steps to deliberately deceive their investors. The truth is somewhere in between. When the mutual fund business was new, nobody knew it would experience the tremendous growth that it has achieved. The investment companies were doing a lot of guessing about performance and whether the concept would even work. They were forecasting marketing expenses without experience or data and marketing a new product (mutual funds) that the public was wary of. The registered representatives were trying to sell something new that was probably a pretty hard sell. These are not excuses for deception, but consultants felt that what they were doing was for the ultimate good of the investor. With the introduction of B, C, and D shares, this type of pricing is no longer necessary. More funds every day are showing market value in dollars, as well as shares, on their statements. I hope that trend continues.

Break points and LOIs are terms used to describe the opportunities investors may have to reduce their commissions by investing larger amounts. Break points usually occur in investment increments of $25,000. If investors are going to invest more than $25,000 or make any investment that will reach another break point within a specified period, they can sign *letters of intent* and pay a commission based on the total dollars they anticipate investing. If clients don't make the required investments within the specified time, their accounts are charged with a commission based on the amount actually invested.

The loads versus no-loads issue has been around since the first funds of either type were sold. It is just as controversial today as it was ten years ago, if not more so. I won't attempt to solve it here. I have discussed the issue somewhat in chapter 4 when I wrote about the value that good financial consultants bring to clients. Some consultants clarify the argument by classifying no loads as *no-service* and loads as *full-service* funds. There is some truth to that description, but it is not that simple. For the beginning financial planner, it may be a major issue of how you enter the business and what type of client relationships you want to develop. If consultants are going to market no-load funds, they must get their money from asset-based or time-based fees. There is nothing wrong with either approach; they just attract a different type of clientele. No-load investors are generally considered more sophisticated and able to make the most of their own investment decisions. However, that is also oversimplified. Often, no-load investors are the most misinformed and invest in no-loads out of fear of being cheated by financial planners. They buy low and sell high because they don't have counseling. Many financial consultants choose to work only with no-loads to reach a level of complete objectivity when it comes to products. My only problem with that limited approach is its omission of well over 50 percent of the products out there, as well as more than half of the available clients. Also, planners must consider the relationships they want with the products they are marketing. No-load advisors want stiff-arm relationships to avoid any appearance of a conflict of interest. Consultants who market load funds may see a highly developed relationship with a mutual fund as a definite advantage for themselves and their clients because of the advanced problem-solving capability, training, and service such a relationship offers.

The issue is a little more cloudy than it used to be because most load funds can now be purchased by money managers without a commission being paid. These are the Y shares I mentioned earlier. This is a confusing part of learning to be a financial planner; you can imagine the *consumer's* confusion. If institutions and money managers can purchase load funds with a commission, doesn't that put the ordinary group 2 and 3 financial consultants and their clients at a disadvantage if they sell the same funds at full commission? Sometimes, but not usually. Most group 2 and 3 financial consultants have access to their own money managers (through their broker-dealers) who can buy the funds at net asset value (no commission). They then charge the clients an asset-based fee. Sometimes the money manager charges clients a fee directly for managing their money, and the financial planner also charges the clients a fee for managing the manager. In other situations, the money manager charges the client a fee and shares this fee with the planner.

Trailers or *trails* are industry buzzwords that are also referred to as 12b-1 fees or account service fees. Relatively rare when I entered the business, they are common today. They usually are paid to the account representative quarterly and range from 10 to 25 basis points. A basis point is a hundredth of a percent. Twenty-five basis points equals one-fourth of 1 percent. Doesn't sound like much when stated that way does it? That is why the industry adopted basis points. One hundred basis points somehow sounds better than 1 percent.

From the perspectives of both consumers and financial consultants, I think that trailers are excellent incentives to help ensure that clients' needs are served by planners. Account service fees pay planners to do just that. From consultants' viewpoints, trailers are an incentive away from transactions and toward relationships. Although 25 basis points doesn't sound like much, an experienced financial planner quickly realizes that they can amount to a lot of income. Quality planners with five or more years of experience should be investing at least $3 million a year for their clients. If that $3 million is subject to trails, then planners will be adding at least $7,500 to their income each year. Ten years of doing this will yield an income of $75,000 in account service fees only, assuming no growth in prior year investments and no other commissions or fees that will be earned on the investments.

Commissions on Securities Sales and Purchases

Usually a small part of group 2 planners' income, these commissions may be a substantial part of group 3's income. Commissions on sales of individual securities vary, and comparisons are hard to make because of minimum costs on some transactions and fees tacked on in others. I think it is safe to say that costs run as low as 0.5 percent to as high as 3.5 percent. Shares bought or sold in odd lots may cost more than those bought in round lots of 100 shares or more. Generally, the larger the purchase, the smaller the percentage commission. Consumers who purchase individual securities usually pay a commission when the security is bought, as well as when it is sold. With mutual funds, the commission is paid only on purchase. This is another reason why selecting individual securities for the small investor should be considered recreation and not financial planning. Group 2 planners will occasionally engage in individual security transactions, but it is usually to sell something that a client already owns so that the money can be repositioned into another investment in accordance with an investment plan.

Payout Schedules

Payout schedules are lists of the percentages of commissions that a broker-dealer pays to its registered representatives. Gross commissions are the amounts that customers pay when they purchase load mutual funds. Gross dealer concession (GDC) is the amount that the mutual fund pays to the broker-dealer on that same transaction. Gross commissions may be the same or less than the GDC. Payout schedules determine the portion of the GDC that the individual registered representative will receive. These percentages may range from 25 to 100 percent. The amount paid is usually based on the production level of the individual registered representative. For wirehouses, the payouts are usually in the lower range because most or all of the representatives' overhead expenses are paid by the broker-dealer. Registered representatives of independent broker-dealers usually have little or none of their overhead expenses covered by the broker-dealer, so their payouts may range from 50 to 100 percent; 100 percent is unusual, but some firms pay out all concessions and charge an annual fee or other related fees. As mentioned previously, payout is only one means of evaluating a broker-dealer; you must first determine what services you want and what you are willing to pay for them.

Insurance and Annuity Products

Annuities generally pay commissions in approximately the same percentages as mutual funds. Fixed annuities can be sold with an insurance license; a securities license is not necessary because fixed annuities are not considered securities. They have no market risk, only credit or interest-rate risk. Their commissions usually range from 3 to 4 percent. Some lower-rated insurance companies may pay higher rates. Variable annuities are considered securities and usually pay from 4 to 6 percent. Many now have trails or allow the broker-dealer to choose between a higher upfront payment or a lower up-front fee with trails.

Traditional insurance products have widely varying commissions. Whole life insurance, universal life, and similar products usually state commissions in terms of percentages of the first year's premiums. Depending on consultants' levels within the insurance sales force, their proven prior production, the proven prior production of their general agents, and their negotiating skills, the planners' payouts can range from 50 to 115 percent of the first year's premium. The general range for financial planners whose primary business is not insurance is going to be 65 percent of the first year's premiums. There are some payments for additional years' premiums but they are minor compared to this first-year commission.

Variable life and variable universal life products are considered securities and must be sold through a broker-dealer. These products are similar to variable annuities, with the addition of life insurance. Their commissions are usually slightly lower than those for traditional insurance products but higher than those for variable annuities. Many other layers of commissions and income opportunities from insurance products exist, with overrides, expense allowances, and other terms used to pay additional bonuses to insurance producers. These commissions vary in amounts and nomenclature with the insurance company, the product being sold, and the state it is being sold in.

Health, disability, and long-term care policies usually pay premiums ranging from 15 to 35 percent of the first year's premium. A much smaller percentage, if any, is paid in future years.

The POP marketing scheme we mentioned in the mutual fund section pales in comparison to the quagmire of misinformation in the insurance industry. In most cases, the clients' money is completely absorbed as soon as they pay the first year's premium. The money goes to the agent or the company. Illustrations show this process, but in a very obtuse and confusing fashion. Illustrations used to sell insurance policies are absurd in their complexity. They have mastered the art of making the simple complex. As with mutual funds, there are reasons for the complexity and the heavy loads in most insurance. A lot of insurance is sold by young salespeople just starting families, and it is hard to sell. The insurance agents may be paid small salaries, but they are usually loans or draws against commissions to be earned. They have to sell policies that pay quickly, which is one of the reasons for the heavy loads. I can understand that approach for small policies, but I don't understand it for huge, estate planning cases. I have no problem with commissions, but I think they are too high on a lot of products and should be leveled out over the premium payment period. Insurance actuaries have excellent arguments about why the policies are written the way they are and why the commissions are the way they are. I don't understand the arguments any better than I do the policies. I am a chartered life underwriter. If I can't understand them, how can the consumer?

Asset-Based Fees

Fees collected as a percentage of assets under management are the most talked-about trend in the industry today. Typical advice at a marketing seminar for financial planners is to go out and gather assets. *Wrap* accounts were first introduced in the late 1980s. Broker-dealers and their registered representatives were offering clients the opportunity to have their money managed for a flat percentage of the value of the account. I think *wrap* referred to several things in the beginning. Clients could get all of their various holdings "wrapped" together under a single reporting system with one report showing everything clients needed to know about all the investments they owned. They could also "wrap" the various transaction fees, commissions, and so forth into one account and pay only a single percentage of assets under management. This percentage depended on the amount of assets under management and on the firm doing the managing. It usually ranged from one half of 1 percent to 3.5 percent annually, payable quarterly. In the frenzy of competition that started with the first wrap account, some of the wrappers got rather flimsy. To make their fees look more competitive, some consultants forgot to wrap in all the fees. The clients would see a ticket charge here and a transaction cost there, in addition to their "all-inclusive" wrap fees. However, they were getting all-inclusive reporting. After some years of settling down, the wrap has taken many forms. *Fee-based advisory services* is a more popular term these days.

Fee-based advisory services can still take many forms. They were first centered only on no-load mutual funds or other individual securities that were purchased for low or no commissions. I have previously written about money managers now being able to buy most load funds at net asset value. This change has considerably broadened the business and brought many other registered representatives into asset-based fees. The new option to use funds where strong relationships already existed has made asset-based fees much more attractive for the traditional registered representative.

Asset-based fees are often difficult for consumers to understand because of the many possible layers. The first layer is the registered representatives or the financial consultants. If they work primarily through their broker-dealers' advisory service or wrap account, then their role is to consult with the client and the personnel who actually run the managed account. They will gather the clients' data and prepare the investment policy statement with the assistance of the broker-dealer personnel. The consultants will also work with the clients and the broker-dealer advisory group to set and implement model portfolios. The people who actually manage the money are usually in the same company as the broker-dealer or a related subsidiary. They constitute the second layer and are responsible for the following:

1. Assisting in the development of the investment policy statement
2. Designing the model portfolio with the planner and the client
3. Implementing the plan by purchasing and repositioning assets as required in the investment policy statement
4. Preparing periodic reports (usually quarterly) for the planner's client
5. Discussing reports with the planner (and the client, if needed)
6. Monitoring and rebalancing or redistributing the investments according to the philosophy of the manager; this could be modern portfolio theory in which investments are redistributed according to the model portfolio designed or could involve market timing or other more aggressive approaches

If the money managers at the broker-dealer are actually selecting securities to buy and sell, then they constitute the last layer. However, they usually select other money managers to manage either part or all of the portfolios. These other money managers could be pure money managers who buy and sell individual securities, or they could be investment companies (mutual funds) or other packaged investment products. These money managers are the third layer. They disclose results to the second layer so that the information can be included in reports prepared by the second layer (money manager at the broker-dealer) for the first layer (registered representatives) to give to their clients. Fees for this type of program usually range from 0.5 to 3 percent.

Confused enough, or should I go into the trust accounts and clearing firms that are also needed? Believe it or not, this process becomes understandable after a few discussions with the second layer and crystal clear when you invest clients' money into fee-based advisory programs. I like to think of it this way: You can manage the client relationship while leaving the accounting, reporting, and management to the second layer, then share in the fees. How much do you share? Usually in the range of 50 to 75 percent. Again, this percentage depends on what other fees are involved, what other relationships you may have with your broker-dealer, and so forth.

If the individual planners want to try it on their own, they can select their own money managers and leave out a layer. However, planners who elect to take this route will need to be much more active not only in terms of managing the client relationship but also in selecting other money managers, choosing individual securities, designing a model portfolio for the client, and carrying out the other six steps mentioned previously. The fourth step is very complex. It includes a lot of accounting work to be sure that all dividends and interest are posted, all share values are current, and so forth.

Some planners elect not to be affiliated with a broker-dealer or use the broker-dealer's advisory service. They may use the services of other major companies that have their own clearing firms and the ability to do transactions and reporting for planners for a fee. The planners then set and retain their own fees.

Time-Based Fees

Many financial consultants charge for their services to clients based on time. Also included in this group are planners who charge fees based on a certain service or level of service. For example, one planner that I know charges $400 minimum for an investment plan that only works with asset allocation. His fee for future consultations is the client's choice of either a retainer of $200 per month or $125 per hour. He charges a minimum of $750 for a partial financial plan that may not include evaluation of insurance or estate planning. His fee for a full-blown financial plan is $2,400. Most planners who charge these types of fees offer them as guidelines when the clients ask, "How much is this going to cost me?" The actual fees may be more but are not usually less. Having practiced this type of planning for about five years, I know that flexibility is necessary because some clients just naturally take a lot more time than others.

As I indicated in chapter 4, myth 2, time-based fees exclude many people. There is nothing wrong with that. Most planners who charge time-based fees only want to work with clients who appreciate their time, value their services, and are willing to cooperate with them on putting together a financial plan. These consultants want to limit the number of clients they serve; I think most planners, including me, have a limited number of clients whom they can effectively manage. However, my personal preference is to have my client base as diverse and as large as possible. This approach might seem to have the effect of diluting the level of service for the highest level of clients, but I found just the opposite to be true. I found that I was better able to provide a high level of service to my clients who required it because of the base of income I had from clients who did not require as much of my time. I also liked the following things about having a large and diverse client base:

1. More referrals
2. Diversity of experience gained; different clients bring different types of problems to be solved and various opportunities for learning
3. Less risk of losing a major portion of income if one or two clients leave; if you have 25 clients and two leave, you could experience an 8 to 10 percent drop in revenue
4. When you are time based, vacation or sick time is very costly
5. There is no cap on your income

Having explained why time-based fees didn't work for me, I still keep them available in my practice for those clients who prefer them. I found that time-based payments are particularly appropriate for clients who may not feel comfortable with a long-term commitment to my services. A client might be moving to another area, for example, but need assistance with a lump-sum distribution today. Some clients may just want guidance in allocating their assets today; they may not be interested in portfolio monitoring or rebalancing, but a buy-and-hold situation. Time-based fees certainly make sense in this environment.

The first major seminar I attended on financial planning was conducted by a pioneer in financial consulting. He was totally time based and said that the maximum number of clients he could possibly handle was 25 and he preferred to work with only ten. I suspect that technology has doubled or even tripled that number today. I don't know the effective number of clients for a time-based planner. I have read of such planners who handle as many as 200 clients.

Many time-based–fee financial consultants do not implement or even get directly involved in the implementation process. They leave that part of the process to others. This method is often used by CPA financial planners who may just prepare financial plans with generic recommendations about portfolio diversification, then refer clients elsewhere. I have been on both sides of these referrals. I used to refer my clients to others for implementation, and I have served many such clients referred from fee-based planners. One client who came as a referral said that he felt like he was left dangling when his plan was not implemented by his first planner.

I implemented these clients' plans but could have done the entire financial planning process for one price and saved them the payment to the fee-only planners. Many other fee-based consultants call in registered representatives and insurance brokers to complete the implementation process. Again, clients pay twice. Also, we have to consider the value of monitoring after implementation. How are fee-based financial consultants who allow others to implement their plans able to effectively monitor the clients' investments after implementation? Financial consultants who base their fees on time and who implement and monitor are the ones who offer their clients true value. Based on my five years of personal experience practicing this type of financial planning and training other financial planners who come from the nonimplementation school, I firmly believe that you must implement and monitor to offer true value to your clients. Today, I believe that most consultants in this group implement and monitor through their own software programs or through the services of clearing firms or companies that offer these services to financial planners.

I suppose a discussion of how financial planners get paid wouldn't be complete without a mention of money managers' (group 1) compensation. Portfolio managers for particular mutual funds within a family of mutual funds are usually paid a salary along with a bonus based on performance. There are also money managers who are not part of investment companies (mutual funds) but who solicit money from investors primarily through group 2 financial planners. They are usually paid some combination of assets under management and bonuses based on performance. Then there are simply independent money managers who manage money for their clients. They are usually paid based on a percentage of assets under management, usually 0.5 to 2.5 percent.

HOW MUCH DO FINANCIAL CONSULTANTS EARN?

If you are considering financial planning as a first or second career choice, you probably want to know how much consultants earn. Of course, I can't answer that question conclusively. Salaried planners' are all over the lot in terms of earnings. I expect that beginning consultants working for a planning firm will make in the high 20s or low 30s with some sort of bonus based on production of plans or overall firm revenue or profits. For salaried personnel with similar experience but who work for investment companies and other larger corporations, earnings will be slightly higher depending on the level of responsibility. Those working for a base salary plus a share of commissions earned or production achieved have the capability to earn much more. Salaries and commissions or production bonuses often go well above $100,000.

Financial planners who want to build their own businesses serving their own clients can expect the earnings based on their levels of experiences shown in Table 8–1. These earning guidelines come from the National Endowment for Financial Education's 1995 survey of CFPs only. The table does not include non-CFPs and many of the broader base of group 3 planners, whose earnings are generally higher.

Instead of just quoting surveys when someone asks me about earnings possibilities, I like to talk about the various ways of making money and how to accumulate earnings. I agree with most pundits that gathering assets is important, but I disagree with some about *why* they are gathered. I believe that most beginning financial planners should gather assets and earn income according to the schedule in Table 8–2. I can safely say that these numbers in the table are achievable for a quality, aggressive financial planner, because they closely parallel those of my own firm.

What do the numbers mean? In the first year, a commission-based financial consultant will make approximately $25,000 in current commissions and a negligible amount of asset service fees or trailers. The planner paid based on assets under management will earn approximately $10,000. In the fifth year, the same commission-based planner will be making $70,000 in current income and approximately $20,000 in trails. The asset-based–fee consultant will earn approximately $80,000. In the tenth year, the respective amounts will be $253,250, with $75,000 in trails vs. $335,000. You can see that the fee- and commission-based planners will make approximately the same amounts. It used to be argued that fee-based planning was superior because the fee-based planners got paid

Table 8–1 Certified Financial Planner Earnings.		
	Gross	**Net**
One to four years experience	$63,500	$45,000
Five to eight years experience or the median	$78,500	$51,000
Nine to twelve years experience	$100,000	$60,000

Table 8–2 Invested Assets Projections.		
	Assets Gathered	
	Current Year	**Cumulative**
Year 1	$1,000,000	$1,000,000
Year 2	$1,250,000	$2,250,000
Year 3	$1,500,000	$3,750,000
Year 4	$2,000,000	$5,750,000
Year 5	$2,500,000	$8,250,000
Year 6	$3,000,000	$11,250,000
Year 7	$4,000,000	$15,250,000
Year 8	$5,000,000	$20,250,000
Year 9	$6,000,000	$26,250,000
Year 10	$7,250,000	$33,500,000

more the better they performed. Prevalence of trails or asset service fees have, in my opinion, lessened the validity of that argument. It is also said that both asset- and time-based fees discourage churning accounts to generate commissions; trails also discourage churning.

With the recent introduction of C and D shares, commission-based financial planners are starting to look more like asset-based–fee managers. After all, a commission is simply a percentage of assets under management. The commission-based planner using C shares now has approximately the same monetary interest in keeping the client invested as the asset-based–fee planner.

What are time-based–fee planners earning in the previous scenario? I don't know. If they are billing at $75 per hour in the first year, they are likely able to bill 30 percent of their time at 60 percent of their target rates. They will gross $27,000. In the fifth year, their billable time should increase to 50 percent. Their rates should increase to $90, and they should hit that rate about 75 percent of the time. If they do, they will make $67,500. In the tenth year, time-based planners should be billing at $115 per hour, hitting the rate about 75 percent of the time, and billing out about 60 percent of their time. They will make $103,500. You can see that the later years are what really separate the two methods.

These comparisons are based on commissioned planners, asset-based–fee planners and time-based–planners who are paid only according to their respective methods. Most planners, I believe, will use some combination of the three types. There will also be a combination of A, B, C, and D shares that will move the numbers around. What I like about this business is that there are so many ways to make money and so many opportunities to build a base so that you don't have to wake up and start over every morning building a new income stream. I think a relaxed financial planner with a strong base income stream bodes well for the client rather than one who is worrying about billable hours.

Good planners will have several automatic bank drafts being done each month, several retirement accounts being invested and several portfolios growing all at the same time. These activities mean more income for the planner with less effort exerted. I think any good businessperson should operate under a formula of energy and reward.

In the beginning, the energy and reward formula is $E = \text{R}$, meaning that huge amounts of energy may be expended for little reward. As the business matures, the formula should reverse to be $\text{E} = R$. Does that mean planners deserve to have incomes that they don't earn or that the clients are still paying when no effort is being expended? The formula doesn't imply any secrecy, just that more effort in the beginning with little reward should equal large rewards in the end with less effort. I think financial consultants who have base income streams to depend on each month will be much more efficient than those who have to worry about doing a certain number of billable hours each month in order to survive.

In this chapter, we have discussed salaries, commissions, asset-based fees, time-based fees, and various combinations of all of them. Which is pure? Which is ethical? Which will do more for the profession? Which method will profit consultants more in the long run? Should that even be a consideration? I have disclosed the path I took, but I do not condemn any other approach. There is no doubt that time-based fees will exclude a large part of the client market for financial-consulting services, which doesn't matter if that is not the market planners want to work with. Because of the layers of managers and resulting expenses in asset-based fees, many less-wealthy clients will also be excluded. Again, it doesn't matter if that's what the planners want and this is the clientele they are prepared to serve. For planners who desire many clients, a broad market, and a wide range of services, my advice is to prepare to be paid in a variety of ways.

9

DISCOVERIES ABOUT PEOPLE AND THEIR MONEY

I learned a lot about people and their money by preparing or reviewing more than 9,000 tax returns over a 20-year period. I also increased my knowledge by doing several hundred financial plans over a 15-year period. In the early days of tax preparation, there were no organizers or prepared forms completed by the client. The most organized of my clients might have envelopes or folders by category. Most, however, fed me information as I asked for it. I knew the questions to ask and they learned to anticipate me. Many questions were answered with "I'll have to get back to you on that." Most questions, however, not only got me answers but a lot more information than I bargained for. People seemed to love to tell me everything about their financial affairs. At first, I didn't want to hear it (unless I could bill them for the conversation). Later, I discovered that I could learn a lot from this volunteered information. People are funny about money. Most don't have a clue about how to reach financial freedom. They feel buffeted by the winds of change, the evolving economy, and the complexity of financial instruments. They have conveniently divided the universe into *haves* and *have nots*. Many have accepted their fates and suffer it gladly. Others are bitter about being cheated by the system. Only a few see an opportunity to control their own destinies when it comes to money. Almost all are misinformed or uninformed. That is why I believe so much in the value and future of this profession.

PROSPERITY CONSCIOUSNESS

Most people don't have it, but do you even know what it is? Prosperity consciousness is a belief system about money that says you can control your own destiny; that your financial future is not in the hands of others, or even in the hands of fate; that you deserve to be prosperous; that you can achieve great financial rewards in more direct methods than winning the lottery; and that your income or wealth level is only limited by the limits you place on it. How do you get prosperity consciousness? Like most things dealing with thinking and awareness, attaining prosperity consciousness is simple in concept and exceedingly difficult in implementation. Some would say that you get it by simply repeating affirmations such as "Money comes to me from many sources for the good of all concerned" or "Wealth comes to me easily." You're probably expecting me to say that these methods are silly, but you may be surprised. I believe that people can change negative thought patterns—about prosperity and other aspects of their lives. However, positive affirmations may not be enough. You must take action to find out where your negative thoughts lie and how to channel them into new positive thoughts. Enter the financial planner.

Financial consultants must get to the heart of problems that are causing clients to have *poverty* consciousness rather than prosperity consciousness. How do they do that? Many answers will come through the data-gathering and questioning phases of the financial planning process. Clients make many comments during questioning that are supplemental to the questions being asked. These comments often hold the clues to how clients think about themselves and money. I have found that it is usually easy to determine which clients see themselves as hopeless victims and which see themselves in control of their financial futures. Some clues are suggested in the following sections.

Is the Client Willing to Be Wealthy?

I know that sounds like a silly question, but many clients simply are not willing to be wealthy. They cannot see themselves as wealthy unless they win the lottery or somehow strike it rich on a get-rich-quick deal. There could be many reasons for this poverty or scarcity consciousness. They may not have much education or be members of a profession. Clients may have parents who were poor or may come from an impoverished area. They may not like their jobs. They may be unhappy in their family lives. They have probably connected wealth to self-esteem, and their self-esteem may be low.

You're probably thinking that financial consultants could easily get in over their heads trying to solve all of these hang-ups. You're right. But remember my admonitions about trying to create a perfect world. You can help clients solve some of these problems. How? By assisting them in articulating and visualizing their goals. By building road maps (financial plans) to reach those goals. By educating and reeducating clients about risks and rewards. By making available investment opportunities they never thought could be available to them. By discussing the negative views listed above and asking simple questions, such as "Why do you feel that way?" and "Why is that important to you?"

How Does the Client View Wealth and Wealthy People?

Most of the things we hear about wealth are negative. Roughly nine out of ten wealthy people we see in movies or in television shows are unsavory or unbalanced characters. I was taught as a child that virtually all wealthy people got that way by cheating someone else. Money was equated with evil and wrongdoing. I didn't realize that this attitude was simply rationalization for the fact that we didn't have any money. It somehow made us feel better to say that we really didn't want it. I overcame that attitude rather quickly by education and observations. Many people, however, take it with them to the grave.

When I started my CPA practice, my new view of wealthy people was affirmed and the teachings of my youth were proven wrong. I saw plenty of wealthy people who had made their money their enemy. Many were afraid to spend it and actually lived in poverty rather than touch it. Many were in constant fear of losing it or doing damage by giving it away. Others were afraid everyone was out to take advantage of them for their money. By and large, however, people with these negative views had inherited their money and felt they didn't deserve it or they had come into the money without actually planning prosperity. Even if they had earned the money, they didn't really feel deserving because they had not planned to be that wealthy. They still had negative thoughts about money.

However, I observed that *most* wealthy people were happy and comfortable with their money. They enjoyed their money and were generous and comfortable with it. They had prosperity consciousness. They had planned their good fortune, felt deserving of it, and enjoyed it to the fullest. They provide a good example to follow. It had little to do with the amount of their wealth or how they attained it; it had everything to do with their states of mind.

Does the Client View the Universe as Opulent or Stingy?

Prosperity-conscious people view the world as an opulent universe. They think that prosperity is available to all people who will follow some rather simple rules and plan for wealth and happiness. Poverty-conscious people have a negative worldview. They prefer affirmations such as "The rich get richer and the poor get poorer," "A working man just hasn't got a chance," or "Money—ain't never had none and ain't never going to have none." Financial planners can change this worldview by asking questions like "What would you do if money were no object? What would you be doing for a living if it didn't matter what you got paid for it?" Ask a lot of questions, listen to the answers, and ferret out the negatives for follow-up questions of "Why do you feel that way?"

Is the Client into Immediate Gratification or Long-Term Rewards?

Most people are into immediate gratification at the expense of long-term rewards. There's nothing wrong with a little immediate gratification, but balance is the key. Balance immediate rewards with visual images and steps toward longer-term, even sweeter rewards. People often view savings and investment as punishment. They don't see it as paying themselves first but as supporting the haggard old men and women that they will become. Why give it to them when we could use it today? They also see money saved or invested as a payment to some "big brother" who will probably tax it completely away before they can enjoy it—hard to argue with that viewpoint. They see things this way because they haven't developed the ability to envision the future as a great place to be. Financial planners can develop this vision by asking questions and painting word images. I have even used graphic images or cut-out pictures in a financial plan to help clients overcome a negative worldview and replace it with a positive vision.

NEVER JUDGE A BOOK BY ITS COVER

Clients come in all types. As discussed previously, they have different views about money and the world in general. It is a financial consultant's job to find out as much as possible about those worldviews and to plan with clients accordingly. I attended a conference once where I heard a speaker (whose name I cannot recall) describe the following money personalities:

> *Hoarders* enjoy delaying gratification. Delaying *becomes* gratification.
>
> *Spenders* can't delay gratification. They love to spend and see saving as punishment.
>
> *Money monks* believe that money will inevitably corrupt them.
>
> *Money avoiders* have a phobia about making financial decisions.
>
> *Money worriers* obsess about their money and need a high degree of control.

Money amassers see money as a game they must somehow win.

Risk takers love the thrill of investing and the potential for high returns.

Risk avoiders are frightened by the possibility of risk.

I have encountered all of these types in practicing accounting and financial planning. Some people combine the various types. I have seen many clients who join the traits of the money monk with the money worrier, for example. On many occasions, one person will be a strong personality of one type and the partner will be strong in another type. This situation requires real work by financial planners. They must get the spouses to try to change roles and role-play past events or even really switch roles for a month for real. They can then appreciate the other's position better. I haven't had much luck in getting clients to go this far, so I am left to empathize, sympathize, and care about each spouse's feelings and try to calm their fears.

Does typecasting clients help in financial planning? I believe that recognizing the various money personalities can certainly help because it keeps consultants from treating everyone the same. It helps us to practice holistic financial planning. Assume you have 12 clients who are all the same age, have spouses who are the same age, children the same age, with the exact same answers on a risk profile. Based on open-ended questions that the planner asks, it is entirely possible that these clients will have 12 different investment portfolio recommendations. It is *probable* that they will have 12 different financial plans.

Typecasting clients can be dangerous if done incorrectly. I have seen planners who incorrectly assumed that clients fit into a type without asking enough questions. In my practice, for example, my most cooperative and rewarding client relationships are often with people I never thought would work with any financial planner, much less me. Most bankers, for example, viewed me as a threat because I was often responsible for clients taking money out of their institutions. However, a bank vice-president and major stockholder in a bank in my community became one of my best clients and referral sources.

There are several small, rural communities surrounding my practice. In fact, my practice is *in* a small, rural community. These surrounding communities are not just small, they are tiny. Many have populations of less than 100. In many of those communities, it was not unusual for me to have five or more clients whose net worth exceeded $1 million. However, if you tried to identify those clients by appearances, you simply could not find them. You won't find them in big houses, driving fancy cars, or wearing designer clothes. Even more surprising, more often than not, they are not in professional occupations. They are not even in high income positions. Most have never had an income exceeding $40,000 per year. *More important, they may not fit exactly into any of the money personalities mentioned previously.*

If I had to classify these people as a group, they started out as money hoarders and risk avoiders. However, further questioning revealed that they were not necessarily hoarding money because *delaying* gratification had *become* their gratification; they were just good stewards of their assets. They lived the lifestyle that was comfortable to them. They often were happy and secure knowing that they were independent. Some, but not all, had suffered during the depression or had parents who did. More often, these people had simply observed other lifestyles that led down roads they didn't want to follow. They were just intelligent, observant people. If they were risk avoiders, it was often because they were lacking education or opportunities to invest outside of things they were familiar with. They kept their money in the assets they had grown up understanding such as banks, cattle, or real estate. A little education on risk and opportunity and a trusting relationship with a financial consultant often led to an even more secure lifestyle, assets that were protected, and a spirit of generosity not possible before.

How do planners deal with these different personalities in the real world? I think the first thing they should do is determine which types they are. If planners know their own types they will learn to rein in their own prejudices and not overreact to clients who are on the other end of the money personality scale. The second thing is to ask open-ended questions. Never let clients control the conversation; especially never let the clients' money personalities control the conversation. Some interpret that to mean that planners should talk all the time. Actually, it means just the opposite. If you are talking all the time, clients are controlling the conversation. In financial consulting, as in most other relationships, the person asking good open-ended questions and *listening* is controlling the conversation. If you let clients vent their frustrations and fears, empathize, and keep asking more questions, they will usually talk themselves out of those fears. If you try to convince them by arguing with them, then they are in control and you are usually going to lose. Even if you win in the short run and convince clients to do something they are not comfortable with, you will eventually lose, because they will not be happy clients.

This area is very tenuous. I believe clients can talk themselves into making changes and overcoming their fears, but I don't believe that planners should do it. I hope you see the difference. It is often difficult to keep control of the conversation with strong-willed clients who want to argue their points. When I lose my train of thought or feel that I am being sucked into an argument, I will use these two basic questions:

"Why is that important to you?" or "What about that is important to you?"

"What does _____ mean to you?" or "What do you mean by _____?" Insert risk, yield, return, or whatever the client is talking about.

Often, the use of these questions will wear thin for clients and me. Then I will restate the positions clients have taken and ask if they could expand on the positions so that I could better understand where they are coming from. The key is to keep clients talking and eventually get them going in the direction you want them to go. When they have talked themselves out, start asking some leading questions that will take clients away from a negative or harmful viewpoint to a more positive one. Caution: It is very easy to appear sarcastic or condescending in these leading questions. If you are not in a caring, sympathizing, or empathizing mode with clients, they will sense it.

One of the most common (and frustrating) experiences I had involved the issue of liquidity. I had a client who had more than $50,000 in a safe-deposit box. He had in excess of $150,000 in his checking account. He was more than 70 years old. When I pointed out all the reasons for moving these assets, he replied, "At my age, you can never tell when I might need my money." I knew that he had a monthly income of more than $15,000, which was roughly triple the amount of his living expenses. He had adequate insurance, and most of his other assets were marketable within 24 hours. It was foolish to have $200,000 lying around drawing no interest. I incorrectly used this language to try to get the client to take action, and I almost lost the client.

That scenario taught me to empathize with clients' feelings and counsel them out of their irrational behavior by asking open-ended questions and providing comfortable solutions. When I approached it from a position of understanding, clients were more receptive to moving away from their fears and irrational acts to more responsible positions. If you simply can't identify in any way with a client's position on money, try to think of another client who felt the same way and the reasons why. When I examined my client's situation by asking more questions, I found it resulted from having had a past emergency and no available cash. Then his situation became understandable.

Don't take clients' attitudes personally. Many clients won't offer up the real reasons for their feelings because they don't fully trust the planner. Also, it not easy to disclose fears unless the planner allows clients a comfortable place to unload. When a financial consultant simply can't empathize, sympathize, or even care about the clients' irrational behaviors with money, it is time to refer those clients to someone else. There are a few people that you can't help. How do you know when that time comes? The barometer I use is when the clients really begin to irritate me or I begin to irritate them. I believe that you can learn to care about someone even when you find their behavior less than appealing and even ridiculous. However, there is a limit to what you can overcome. There is a time for both client and planner to move onto more productive relationships.

THE THIRTEEN MOST COMMON MISTAKES THAT INVESTORS MAKE

Through observation and notes, I have found that my clients make certain mistakes repeatedly. As I list these mistakes, note how the role of a good financial consultant could have prevented them all.

1. Meandering through life without goals or strategies. The obvious solution is sitting down with a good financial planner and devising a financial plan.
2. Failing to understand the various types of risk and that some risk is necessary and even good. One solution is getting educated about the risk-reward principle and how different types of risk affect even the safest investments.
3. Investing in hot tips and get-rich-quick schemes. (Texas had its first lottery only a short time ago, and the response was tremendous.) A solution is education from a good financial consultant about how to get rich slowly or methodically and learning that high-risk investing should be viewed only as recreation, not financial planning.
4. Searching for the perfect investment. Financial planners should not practice paralysis by analysis. If consultants fall into this trap, why should they not expect paralysis to affect clients also? Teach clients that the perfect investment does not exist; then find out which of its attributes are most important to them.
5. Following the crowd mentality by investing at the top and selling at the bottom. This kind of behavior is repeatedly exhibited by individuals who are into self-help financial planning. Good planners counsel their clients away from these normal tendencies.
6. Putting all eggs into one basket. In their search for the perfect or most comfortable investment, people often seize on one statement or phrase made by a person they admire and invest all of their assets into that one thing. Many emotions drive this type of behavior: the need for understanding and simplicity, the need to believe in something, the need for control, and the need to get rich quick. Good financial consultants will explain modern portfolio theory in terms that clients can understand. Diversification reduces risk and increases the probability of a higher return over long periods.
7. Not seeking help when it is needed. Most people don't see themselves as clients of financial planners. Seeking out a trusting relationship is time-consuming and can be frus-

trating. Good financial planners will put themselves in as many positions of communication as they can to show that a relationship with a financial consultant can be non-threatening and beneficial.

8. Investing or saving sporadically without discipline. People act based on emotion. When they feel good about planning for the future, they invest or save. When they need instant gratification, they spend and do not save. Financial consultants can put these clients on automatic investment programs that bring discipline to their lives.

9. Falling for sensation and fear stories told by the media, politicians, or unscrupulous advisors. Good financial consultants will use discomfort, not fear, as a motivator. Good planners counsel clients through irrational fears.

10. Drowning in a sea of liquidity or having no liquidity. Clients usually have too much or too little liquidity. They may have a year's income in a checking account or safe-deposit box, or they may have no emergency fund at all. Good financial planning relationships will discover the cause for these contrasting needs and bring balanced liquidity. It may lead to a plan with good liquidity or it may just be a process of educating clients about the differences between liquidity and marketability or long-term values of liquid investments and not-so-liquid investments. Clients may be allowed to have their little stashes of cash in some cases, but only in moderation.

11. Not recognizing the ninth wonder of the world. Most clients don't understand the miracle of compounding. It is just arithmetic, but most have never had it quantified and related to their personal situations. I will usually make projections for clients using various rates of return with various investments over various periods. I put the numbers on a flip chart or on their own notepads to take home. They are usually amazed at what small steps can accomplish over a long enough period.

12. Investing only money—not time and money. Clients must be educated to invest time and money into their investments, and they must be taught this up front. Use the

techniques in the eleventh mistake to get this message across. If clients are into instant gratification, they must be taught that time is their friend when it comes to investments. A good financial plan is the best teacher I have found.

13. Investing what is left. I know it is a cliché, but paying yourself first works. Most people won't budget. Don't expect clients to do something that you won't do yourself. The best budget is one that automatically invests something when the paycheck arrives rather than waiting to see if there is anything left at the end of the month, which there seldom is.

NAPOLEON HILL'S SIX STEPS THAT TURN DESIRES INTO GOLD

Author of the best seller *Think and Grow Rich* (1966), as well as several other books, Napoleon Hill could be considered the founder of prosperity consciousness. His six steps that turn desire into gold foretold the advent of the financial planning industry. I often use his books and those of other authors to illustrate points to clients and other financial consultants. The following are his steps. Note how closely they parallel the financial planning process.

1. Fix in your mind the exact amount of money you desire.
2. Determine exactly what you intend to give in return for the money you desire.
3. Establish a definite date when you intend to possess the money you desire.
4. Create a definite plan for when you intend to possess the money you desire.
5. Write out a clear, concise statement of the amount of money you intend to acquire, name the time limit for its acquisition, state what you intend to give in return for the money, and describe the plan through which you intend to accumulate it.
6. Read your written statement aloud twice daily, once just before retiring at night, and once after arising in the morning. As you read—*see and feel and believe yourself already in possession of the money* (1966, p. 36).

THE NINE STAGES OF MASTERY OVER MONEY

Stage 1   Blissful Ignorance

Babies, we are not aware that money is even an issue in our lives.

Stage 2   Spending

Money becomes an issue because we know that it will buy things. This occurs at about age 4 or 5 and continues into the teens. Some people never outgrow it.

Stage 3   Earning and Spending

Most people at this stage have started to earn money and recognize that money is an issue not only because it will buy things, but because someone has to earn it in order to buy more things. Usually this is the teenage stage or early twenties.

Stage 4   Afraid and Ignorant

People in this stage are usually fresh out of the nest or protection of a parent or other support mechanism. They know that not only is money an issue because it will buy things, but also because it is necessary for survival. These people have often found themselves running out of money before they run out of month. They may have experienced the painful moment when they are out of or short on food. They may have been late with the rent and actually faced the possibility of being without shelter.

Stage 5   Some Knowledge, More Fear

People at stage 5 have recognized that knowledge about money and how to get it could be important to survival. Many have asked friends or relatives about money. A subscription to a magazine about money or the economy could have entered the picture. They know enough to recognize real trouble and may be more afraid than in stage 4. Life is not as simple as it was, and it is not going to get any simpler.

Most people get stuck in this stage. If they are going to get stuck here, they adopt a passive attitude that the world is going to get them anyway and stop fighting it. They will continue to be buffeted around by economic winds and will often lead lives of quiet desperation. Some go into denial and try to regress to stage 3 or even stage 1 or 2. They first deny that money is important. Then they may start to resent money, anyone who has any, and all the things it stands for.

Those wishing to progress to stage 6 start to fight and accumulate more knowledge. They start to save and even invest. These people are not going to give up without a fight. A financial planner may enter the picture here.

Stage 6   Accumulation and Learning

People in this stage have recognized and accepted that *if it is to be, it is up to me.* They have taken positive steps to accumulate investments and to learn more about financial planning. Those who reach this stage almost always progress to stage 7. However, they are still precariously perched in this stage. Health problems, job loss, divorces, deaths in the family, and other problems can send them falling back to stage 5 and lower. Any step back can start a fast decline. Those who progress are well into a regular investment program. They are starting to fight back, but still feel out of control. They are willing to learn more, however. These people make excellent financial planning clients.

Stage 7   Choices

People at stage 7 have accumulated enough assets to feel the wonderful freedom of choice in such things as homes to live in, cars to drive, clothes to wear, and vacations to take. The more advanced in stage 7 may look at the real possibility of early retirement or a second career. Their realm of possibilities has expanded and they begin to think creatively if they are going to advance to stage 8. Only the worst calamity can shove them back to stage 5 or below. If a financial setback sends them to stage 6, they have enough knowledge and confidence to recover.

Many remain or become money amassers or risk takers at this stage, however. They feel powerful and make the wrong choices if they do not seek proper advice. They often spend the rest of their lives in this stage or between stages 6 and 7. Those who go to stage 8 usually recognize what financial planning has accomplished for them and are eager and experienced students of the process.

Stage 8   Freedom

Some level of financial security has been reached. Stage 8 people are no longer constrained in their thinking; they can and usually do consider alternate career possibilities, taking a year or longer sabbatical, turning hobbies into fun careers, starting creative endeavors, buying or building second homes, or moving to an alternate location. If a career has become boring or even nonchallenging, leaving the career is an easy choice. There is enough money to support a comfortable lifestyle without working again.

Some people who reach stage 8 are able to relax and enjoy the fruits of their labors. They usually go onto stage 9 because they have begun to attract money. Earning it is no longer difficult, but amazingly easy and usually fun.

Many people who reach this stage, however, do not recognize the choices they have. Their freedom often came from a very difficult and challenging career path. They do not see their freedom as having come from planning, but hard work, taking risk, and playing the game. They often remain risk takers and money amassers. The worst cases evolve into monks, avoiders, and worriers. They have freedom but do not enjoy it and may fall back to very low stages in their thinking. I have some clients who qualified for stage 8 in terms of assets but remained in stage 5 in their thinking.

Stage 9   Freedom, Balance, and Generosity

At this stage, people have reached the top of the mountain. Money is no longer an issue. Their existing assets and developed character traits attract people and circumstances that increase the level of their freedom and generosity. They have more than enough assets and income to live a balanced and happy lifestyle. They have usually lost their need to accumulate things, but have acquired a great love for helping others. They freely and happily share their physical and spiritual wealth with their families and with those people and causes they deem worthy. It is rare for anyone to ever fall from stage 9.

The discoveries I made about people and their money were invaluable to me in building a solid financial planning practice. I have used them repeatedly in training other financial consultants. During the discovery process, I learned much about my own money personality and how I can use that information to help clients. Uncovering your own fears and those of your clients is an integral part of becoming a quality financial planner. Once they are exposed and dealt with, you can move away from fear and toward the secure feeling that comes with having purpose in your life and reaching the final stage of mastery over money.

10

FINANCIAL PLANNING 2015 AND A FEW FINAL WORDS

Where will financial planning be in the year 2015? I like writing about the future because it is an open subject. Except for the fact that I am not trained as a futurist, my opinion is as good as anyone else's. Who is going to prove me wrong? If I am wrong, my predictions will be long forgotten by the time two decades roll by. Who can remember today what the prophets said would happen during 1996? I don't really know where financial planning will be in the year 2015, but I have some ideas.

During the 1995 Institute of Certified Financial Planners Retreat, the keynote address was given by Jennifer Jones, a cultural anthropologist (one who specializes in cultural change). She said that the American society is in the midst of chaos. She compared the cultural change we are undergoing today to the agricultural and industrial revolutions, except that it is much broader, deeper, and happening much more rapidly. Call it the technological revolution. It is already broad and deep today, and it is certainly happening rapidly. Sixteen years ago, I bought my first personal computer. Before owning this PC, my only experience with a computer had been in large, environmentally controlled rooms with false floors for cables to run under. The rooms were populated with people wearing white smocks. They spoke a language I didn't understand and visibly enjoyed everyone else's confusion about what they did. I showed the proper respect for their superiority, because I had no idea that most of them had little or no idea of what they were doing either. That was in the early 1960s. Only a few had electronic calculators then. I had no computer training through 16 years of education, and I managed to maintain my innocence about automation for about three years after college. Then I was forced to start using the information supplied by the data-processing department of the company I worked for. I was thankful that I still did not have to actually operate those awful machines.

When I bought that first PC in 1981, I knew I had to learn at least the basics about it before I passed it off to staff members. About the time I became an expert user of electronic calculators, I also became a computer novice. I knew I was buying a machine that would eventually replace me. It would change forever the nature of the services I rendered, the demand for them, and their price. I was only a little worried in 1981, because I figured I would probably be retired before it got too serious. After all, the huge monstrosity they called a personal computer with its printer cost me well over $25,000. It was unreliable and difficult to use, unless you liked fixing problems hourly. How many of my clients would buy one of these things? Three years later, the things were taking over my business. They had not robbed me of many clients yet, but they were certainly transforming me from a professional to a machine operator.

When prices came down, I predicted that thousands of computers would be bought only to sit in closets unused. People would not be able to effectively use the software on the market for many practical purposes. I was right. However, I didn't predict that there would also be millions that were used extensively and that software would become so cheap and friendly that anyone could use it only a short time later.

It was only a few years ago that we nontechnical types first heard of the information superhighway. Even today, most of us have only an inkling as to how the World Wide Web affects our daily lives. *Internet* is not in most dictionaries and is certainly not identified by my word processing dictionary as I write this book. I never believed that so many people would be "surfing the net." I did not predict that political candidates would have their own web sites and a lot of television programs would have electronic addresses. I certainly could not have predicted that technology would give me the opportunity to play a key role in building a company without leaving my home office to visit the headquarters more than once a week.

Before I started enjoying the benefits, I really considered technology my enemy. It was making life too complicated. Things were going too fast. Technology was making it possible for my clients to do things with software that only I could do for them before. It was going to destroy my business. It was changing a seasoned professional into a rookie. I think that negative view of technology is shared by many people. However, as soon as they see their personal lives benefiting by its use, it will become an ally, a friend. When people see their kids using it, technology may become a close friend. This transformation is happening as I write, and it is happening fast. The computer I am writing this book on was bought less than a year ago and is already outdated.

What does technology mean to financial planning as a profession? Is technology the great equalizer that some pundits claim it to be? Will we be a nation of do-it-yourself financial planners? Will financial plans be prepared at home by software that asks you a few questions and then spits out a plan for you? Will you be able to purchase any mutual fund or security you want through a simple dial-up on the Internet? Many of these options are already available. The next question is when it will be economical and practical to use for ordinary people. When will they want to use it? I don't know the answer. I have already admitted to a failing in the prognostication department.

I know it is probably not an apples-to-apples comparison, but I can also remember when the first televisions came into homes. Futurists were predicting that all sorts of things would happen to our lives as a result. Television did bring about vast changes in our lives. In the late 1950s, some said that we would soon be purchasing most of our products from television screens. Almost 40 years later, we are buying some products through television, but far from most. The technological revolution has rendered vast changes in our lives and there is little doubt that it will create more. If you resist too long, you may be run over. Jennifer Jones also said that "the nerds will inherit the earth," because they use energy more efficiently than the rest of us—the renewable resource of the human mind, tied into the computer.

Are all nontechnical people going to have to become nerds or get left behind? I don't think so, but we will have to change our points of reference. If technological advancement worries you in this profession, it will probably worry you in any other. I can't think of many people who won't be affected by it. However, if you reframe your reference and see technology as a nonthreatening friend, it will probably help you in this profession more than it will hurt you. Just like some of the predictions about television's impact, I expect that many of the changes will happen, but many will not. Just because we are not out on the bleeding edge of technology doesn't mean we can't use it to our advantage. We don't have to be the first to use it but must use it well and practically. Use common sense and stay agile and alert. Change when you are ready and when you feel it will benefit your clients.

Even as we move into this new world, I think money will still be the medium of exchange and the resource of choice. One of the great things about this business is that we can practice financial planning on ourselves. If we follow our own advice, we will be in stage 9 of mastery over money, and it won't matter. We are in a great position to see that both we and our clients arrive safely at stage 9.

I keep a couple of signs in my office that summarize my philosophy. The first states investment philosophy. It has four basic points.

1. Establish and keep an emergency fund
2. Invest—don't just save—regularly
3. Invest for and think long term
4. Diversify

I have another sign that offers this sage advice:

For the unprepared, old age can truly be the winter of life
For the prepared, it is the season of harvest

Really technical stuff. I like for things to be stated simply.

Are we a profession of complexity or simplicity today? In 2015? I recently read a response to an article that was written in a leading industry publication. The author of the first article is reported to have said, "Today, the classical capital ideas are suspected of suffering from kurtosis, skewness, and other less familiar malignancies. They are under attack from nonlinear hypotheses, overwhelmed by fears of discontinuities rather than pricing volatility." The article went on to say that at least one leader in our profession believes that we should understand and be able to explain that paragraph in toto to our clients or we shouldn't be charging them for managing their money. My first response was "nonsense." Then I realized that I was doing the same thing that this industry leader had. I was choosing my own definition of money management and coming down rigidly on the side of simplification based on my own experiences. His definition of charging for money management and the value good consultants bring to their clients is obviously different than mine. His clients are also different than mine. If I start talking about skewness, kurtosis, and nonlinear hypotheses on a regular basis to my clients, I am certain that I would be committing professional suicide. I see no need to talk to them in those confusing terms. It seems that if clients are interested in such technical hypotheses, they don't really need a financial planner. They may need money managers, but I doubt that as well. Obviously the person who voiced this opinion has clientele who wish to talk in these terms. Surely he wasn't just showing off.

Are consultants simple or complex today and in 2015? Would it be cowardly to say both? I truly believe the most successful financial consultants in America today practice the basics of the business much more often than they practice the fringe technicalities. I can say that with some authority because I take every opportunity to hear them speak or to talk with them. Consultants consistently speak about the same things over and over, and those same things are generally pretty simple. I don't mean to imply that you can or should remain ignorant of the technicalities of this profession. You must become familiar with them in order to serve a wide range of clients. Again, the key is balance. Balance your technical skills with your people and relationship skills and your product skills. Don't get hung up on one or the other or you are going to wind up with your nose in the air and your head in the clouds. Stay aware of what is happening around you and what your clients need from you. Then go out and get it and deliver it to them.

Technology will probably make the business simpler rather than more complex. If you want to do a nonlinear hypothesis mixed with a little skewness and kurtosis, for example, it will probably have its own little icon. Someone once said, "All of my best ideas were stolen by the ancients." That comment had to sink in for a few minutes, but it is so meaningful. Most really great ideas and discoveries have already been taken by wise people from the past. The nice thing is that we get to discover them again with each generation.

How can I summarize my conclusions and best advice for someone who aspires to be a financial consultant? Some of you may be old enough to remember Dustin Hoffman in *The Graduate.* As a recent college graduate, he was at a dinner party sponsored by his parents to celebrate his graduation. One of the mature, obviously successful gentlemen in attendance whispered one word in his ear: plastics. I would like to whisper a similar meaningful one word of advice in your ear about this profession and the pages that precede. Would you settle for a few phrases instead?

> Common sense—Hopefully, you have it. Listen to that inner voice if it makes sense. Even if it is different from your academic studies, the inner voice is probably right.
>
> Balance—Next to love, it is my favorite word. I have used it many times in this book. Strive for balance in all things. Don't be rigid and inflexible. Financial planning is a recipe that involves many ingredients. Each client engagement is the same way. Learn to balance your ingredients.
>
> Practice—You have to practice to be good at most things. Financial planning is no exception. I don't suggest that you plunge in but that you start working in real situations as soon as possible. Your studies for a professional designation will be greatly enhance if you are applying the knowl-

edge as soon as you receive it. Remember my admonition to fake it till you make it. You can't become something overnight without practice. Also, practice what you preach. Take your own medicine.

Empathy, sympathy, and caring—These are skills, as well as attitudes. You can develop them. You must feel them and learn to get inside your clients' heads and hearts.

Buy and hold—It's not getting much talk these days, but all things run in cycles, including theories about money management and financial planning. This method is appropriate for some clients today. Rebalancing may yield better results, but there are prices to pay.

Diversify—Diversifying reduces risk while increasing your chances for a better return. It is probably better known as *asset allocation.*

KISS—Your clients will like you better if you Keep It Short and Simple.

Respect—Respect yourself and your clients. If you can't respect them or they can't respect you, the relationship isn't working.

Relationships—More than anything else, financial consulting is about relationships. It is difficult to really care about someone you do not know. Obviously, you cannot know everything about any client. However, when you are able to hear or experience another person's fears, hopes, dreams, and aspirations, and share your own, a relationship is created. The honesty, integrity, and health of that relationship is determined by the degree to which we can reveal ourselves honestly to the other, and the honest responses that we receive.

Appendix A

Contact Listing
for Professional Licenses
and Credentials

Certified Financial Planner (CFP)

National Endowment
for Financial Education (NEFE)
4695 South Monaco Street
Denver, CO 80237-3403
(303) 220-1200 or (303) 220-4800
or
College for Financial Planning
1660 Lincoln Street #3050
Denver, CO 80264
(303) 830-7543

Chartered Financial Consultant (ChFC)

The American College
P.O. Box 1513
270 South Bryn Mawr
Bryn Mawr, PA 19010-2195
(610) 526-1490

American Institute of Certified Public Accountants–Personal Financial Specialist (AICPA–PFS)

The American Institute of
Certified Public Accountants
Personal Financial Specialist
Division
1211 Avenue of the Americas
New York, NY 10036-8775
(212) 596-6142

Chartered Life Underwriter (CLU)

The American College
P.O. Box 1513
270 South Bryn Mawr
Bryn Mawr, PA 19010-2195
(610) 526-1490

Chartered Financial Analyst (CFA)

Association for Investment
Management and Research
P.O. Box 3668
Charlottesville, VA 22903
(804) 977-6600

Certified Investment Management Analyst (CIMA)

Investment Management
Consultants Association
9101 East Kenyon Avenue
Suite 3000
Denver, CO 80237
(303) 770-3377

Certified Fund Specialist (CFS)

Institute of Fund Specialists
7911 Herschel Avenue
Suite 201
La Jolla, CA 92037-4413
(619) 454-4073
or 1-800-858-2029

Chartered Mutual Fund Counselor (CMFC)

National Endowment
for Financial Education
4695 South Monaco Street
Denver, CO 80237-3403
(303) 220-1200

Registered Investment Advisor

Each state has different registration requirements. Contact your
state securities department or
board and ask for the division
that handles RIA inquiries. Alternately, you may contact your
broker-dealer for further information.

Master of Science Degree Program

National Endowment
for Financial Education
College for Financial Planning
Attn: Marketing Department
4695 South Monaco Street
Denver, CO 80237-9811

Appendix B

NASD and Insurance Exams

NASD Series 6: Investment Company and Variable Contracts

The NASD Series 6 exam is for consultants who will offer investment company products such as mutual funds or who will sell variable annuity contracts and variable life insurance. The Series 6 exam alone will not qualify you to sell both mutual funds and insurance products in most states. Most states also require the Series 63, as well as the Series 6, to sell mutual funds. To sell variable insurance products, you must also hold an insurance license. Licensing requirements for insurance vary by state.

    The exam is 100 questions and two hours, fifteen minutes in length. You must have a grade of 70 percent or better to pass. Exams are offered daily in most major metropolitan areas.

NYSE Series 7: General Securities Registered Representative

This is the strongest of all the securities exams in that it covers equities, fixed income and government securities, municipals, options, and limited partnerships. The exam is for those who want to be able to offer a full array of products. The same rules as indicated previously for the Series 6 apply: most states also require the Series 63 and you must have an insurance license to sell variable insurance products.

The exam is 250 questions in two three-hour sessions. A grade of 70 percent or better is required to pass. Exams are offered daily in most major metropolitan areas.

NASD Series 63: Uniform Securities Agent State Law Exam

Individual states sometimes require this exam as a condition of registration. It is currently required in 41 states. The exam covers the Uniform Securities Act and provides guidelines for state registration of securities. The exam is 50 questions and you are given 60 minutes. A grade of 70 percent or better is required to pass. Exams are offered daily in most major metropolitan areas.

Insurance Licenses

Most states have different rules for obtaining an insurance license. As a rule of thumb, one exam will allow you to sell traditional life insurance, fixed annuities, health insurance, and disability insurance. In Texas, this is called a group 1 license. Some states require a second exam (in addition to the Series 6 or 7) to sell variable insurance. Some only require the submission of a separate application showing that you hold the group 1 license or its equivalent along with a Series 6 or 7.

Broker-Dealers

Anyone who sells a financial product classified as a security must be sponsored by a broker-dealer. An initial relationship must be established in order to be sponsored for taking the NASD or NYSE exams. Listing all of the broker-dealers would take several dozen pages. However, you can go to the public library and ask for the *Securities Dealers of North America* reference book. This is a red book and can be used for reference only, but not checked out. It lists broker-dealers alphabetically by state, then by city, and then by broker-dealer. It offers brief descriptions of the type of securities each provides but does not describe the type, that is, discount, full service, wirehouse, or independent. For the latest industry survey on broker-dealers compiled by industry periodicals, contact me at the following address:

1st Global Capital Corp.
12700 Hillcrest
Suite 175
Dallas, Texas 75230

Exam Study Materials

There are many qualified organizations that provide excellent study materials in all types of formats and methods of learning. You can do home study, classroom study, computer program study, and so forth. Many broker-dealers also have their own study materials or arrangements to obtain discounted study materials from other sources. These sources are familiar to me:

Securities Exam Preparation, Inc.
P.O. Box 32
Haugan, MT 59842
1-800-648-7277

Education Training Systems, Inc.
National Endowment for Financial Education
Student Service Center
4695 South Monaco
Denver, CO 80237-3403

Investment Companies (Mutual Funds) Information

Investment Company Institute
1401 H. Street, NW
Washington, DC 20005-2148
(202) 326-5600 or (202) 326-5971
or
P.O. Box 27850
Washington, DC 20038-7850

Appendix C

Sample Financial Plan*

John B. and Susie Q. Average

The following sample financial plan is for a couple with two children. Personal and financial data have been gathered by the financial consultant before preparing the plan. The husband is age 40 with an annual income of $45,000. The wife is age 42 with an annual income of $60,000. They have two children—Jerry, age 9, and Holly, age 7. Based on a series of risk profile questions, the planner and the clients have agreed that their risk tolerance is medium. They are reasonably good savers but do not have a disciplined investment program. They have bought some individual shares of stock before and a few mutual funds through a broker but have never actually had a plan prepared before.

John, the husband, is employed as a middle management executive at a printing company. Susie, the wife, is a senior executive with a large department store chain. They both consider their positions to be secure for the long term and both have good educations

*This information is provided as an example only. Although based on real client situations, this sample financial plan does not include standard engagement letters, disclaimers, or disclosure statements generally included in specific financial plans prepared by the author.

with marketable skills. Both have recently had substantial pay increases that will allow them additional disposable income they have not enjoyed before (approximately $15,000). Also, they have recently decided independently that they wish to adjust their lifestyles from consumption oriented to savings oriented. This should free up an additional $10,000 per year.

The plan should begin with a cover page, which could look like this:

A PERSONAL
FINANCIAL/INVESTMENT PLAN

Prepared especially for

<u>John & Susie Q. Average</u>

December 1996

Consultant Name

Name of Company

The next box should list the contents of the plan, for example:

CONTENTS

1   Your Goals

2   Plan Summary

3   Assets Available to Meet Your Goals

4   Assets Required to Meet Your Goals

5   Estate Projections

6   Insurance Needs

7   Our Recommendations

Step 1: **Your Goals**

This is just a restatement of the goals the client provided to you in the data gathering process. Obviously, you do not show any other goals on the form. Just your client's stated goals. If you are only working on an education fund, then that will be the only goal shown. Remember, this is a customized plan.

When you set up the client goal sheet, print it and put it in plain sight all of the time you are working on the plan. When presenting the plan to the client, reread the goals and ask:

> "Are we in agreement that these are the goals you are trying to reach?"

Here is a sample goal sheet:

John B. and Susie Q. Average

Your Goals

1. To be financially independent at John's age 60 with an annual income of $50,000 in today's dollars
2. To accumulate enough funds to pay for Jerry and Holly's education at state university
3. To provide funds for weddings for both children
4. To protect our assets and income stream to ensure we reach our goals
5. To build a small house in the country to use as a second home before Susie reaches age 50

Step 2: **Plan Summary**

I like to do a plan summary up front. It goes with my belief in

1. telling what you are going to tell them,
2. telling them,
3. telling them what you told them.

It is easy to confuse the summary with the recommendations at the end of the plan. The summary is more of a sequential step process for all of the things that the client needs to do to reach his goals. The recommendations are usually arranged in order of the goals stated and are more detailed than the summary. The summary may cover several steps included in the recommendations. Again, if possible, I like to have the summary steps stated in **sequential order.**

Depending on the type of client you are dealing with, the summary sheet, the recommendation sheet, or both may be the only sheets necessary to discuss with the client. If your client is a get-to-the-point type of person, then go with the summary. If the client is more analytical, then you may need to go over the plan page by page. I recommend starting with the summary. Watch the client's reactions, then proceed accordingly.

The plan summary may be presented like this:

John B. and Susie Q. Average
Financial Plan
December 1996

Plan Summary

In the following pages, I have included specific recommendations with supporting schedules that should start you on the path to achieving your goals as stated. As we agreed, these recommendations represent beginning steps toward financial freedom. They must be reviewed at least annually; more often if your circumstances change. Also, they should be reviewed if major shifts in markets or interest rates occur. Please notify me of any plans that your employers may have to allow you to shelter your income inside retirement plans.

To reach your goal of financial freedom and the ability to retire at John's age 60, I have recommended the investment of $15,600 per year into a portfolio of mutual funds and a variable annuity that should match your risk and personality profiles. The variable annuity will also contribute toward the plan of diversifying assets and tax deferral. The monthly investments have been allocated toward achieving the best return possible with the minimum level of risk you have indicated to be acceptable.

To reach your goal of educating the children, I have recommended the setup of Uniform Transfer to Minor accounts for each child. Investing $500 per month total into these funds should provide the necessary funds for their college educations. For this type of investment, I have recommended aggressive growth funds. Although these funds alone would exceed the level of risk you have indicated, I think they will best achieve our objective in the time frames we have with the most favorable tax consequences. Also, you have more conservative investments in other recommendations for balance and diversification.

(continued)

(*continued*)

　　To provide for weddings for the children, I have recommended the same accounts be used to fund your $90 per month investment.

　　For your goal of protecting your assets and income streams, I have recommended minimal increases in your levels of both life and disability protection. Per your instructions, the recommendations are based on minimal coverages in order to conserve funds for achieving the first three goals.

　　To achieve your fifth goal of building a second home, I have recommended some changes and combinations of your existing investments and savings that should accomplish this goal.

　　In summary, our prior meetings and analysis showed approximately $25,000 annually that would be available for reaching your goals. This is to be provided by recent increases in salaries for each of you ($15,000) and by changing spending habits ($10,000). The money is to be allocated as follows:

Goal # 1	Financial independence at John's age 60	$15,600
Goal # 2	Children's educations	6,000
Goal # 3	Children's weddings	1,080
Goal # 4	Income and asset protection	2,320
Goal # 5	Build a second home (to be funded with existing assets)	0
Total		$25,000

Step 3: Assets Available to Meet Your Goals

　　This can be just a nicely printed version of the Statement of Financial Condition completed as part of data gathering. I don't usually include the detail schedules as part of the plan but keep the list available for reference. For analytical types, I may include the detailed lists. Often, it is supplemented with assets *separately listed* that are applicable to this plan only. For example, if the client's stated goal for this plan only is to retire at age 60 with an annual income of $50,000, you would only include assets available for this purpose on the list. Education funds, personal residence, auto, and so forth would not be included because they will not be available to meet this goal.

This is the starting point. It brings both you and your client to a focus point of where you are starting from. It helps both of you understand the distance that must be traveled to reach your goals.

Here are two sample schedules:

John B. & Susie Q. Average
December 1996

What We Own

Productive Assets
  Liquid Assets

Cash (1)	$ 3,460	
Certificates of deposit (2)	78,400	
Stocks (3)	3,642	
Bonds (4)	—	
Mutual funds (5)	8,453	
U.S. Gov't Securities (6)	—	
Life Insurance Cash Values (7)	2,465	
Total liquid assets		$96,420 [A]

  Nonliquid assets

Loans receivable (8)	—	
Rental property (9)	—	
Other real estate (10)	—	
IRAs (11)	48,000	
Other retirement accounts (12)	—	
Practice/business value (13)	—	
Total nonliquid productive assets		48,000 [B]
Total productive assets [A + B]		$144,420 [C]

Personal Assets

Home (15A)	165,000	
Vacation home (15B)		
Home furnishings (15C)	6,000	
Automobiles (15D)	32,000	
Other personal assets (15E)	12,000	
Total personal assets		$215,000 [D]
Total nonliquid assets [B + D]		263,000 [E]
Total Assets [A + E] or [C + D]		$359,420 [F]

John B. & Susie Q. Average
December 1996
What We Owe
Home Mortgage (A-1) $ 84,000 [G]
Other Real Estate
     Vacation home (A-2)   —
     Rental Property (A-3)   —
     Other (A-4)   —
     Total other real estate   — [H]
Auto Loans: [B]   12,000 [I]
Credit Cards/Installment Loans [C]   4,000 [J]
Other Debt
     Other secured debt [D]   —
     Business and investment
       obligations [E]   —
     Other life insurance cash
       value loans [F]   —
     Other [G]   —
     Total other debt   — [K]
Total Liabilities [G through K] $100,000 [L]
Net Worth Calculation
     Total assets $359,420 [F]
     Total liabilities (-)   100,000 [L]
     Net worth [F - L] $259,420 [M]

Step 4: Assets Required to Meet Your Goals

This section is a critical part of almost any plan prepared, from the smallest to the largest. It tells the client and you the funds necessary to gather before the client's goal can be obtained.

A. Funds Required

For each goal stated by the client, you must be able to quantify as much as possible the assets that must be accumulated to reach the goal. For example, if a client's goal is to educate an 11-year-old daughter, you must be able to determine the approximate amount of college costs in seven years. If the client has a good idea of where the daughter will go to school, then you can obtain the information easily. Several of the mutual fund sponsors provide specific college cost information, often the parents will know the cost, or you can make a call to the university. Once you know today's cost, you can easily project the cost in seven years using an assumed inflation rate and your financial calculator or one of the many software programs available. You can determine the monthly savings required the same way.

B. Determining Living Expense Needs

We will include a separate schedule for this as part of the plan only if it is critical to the client's goals, or if retirement is imminent or if the client is facing a loss of her job.

C. Financial Security Planning Worksheet

I use this form in almost every financial plan that involves any type of investment toward retirement. Even if the client is not retirement minded, I believe it is prudent to point out the funds that may be required to have a secure retirement. The amounts are very surprising to most people.

This form is important enough to warrant line-by-line instructions.

1. Current Annual Living Expense Needs

If you completed a "Determining Living Expense Needs" form or an Income Statement for the year form, then fill in the amounts determined. If not, I just use the tax return to estimate what the clients are spending. If you are working with long-range goals, I think it is permissible to just use adjusted gross income from the tax return for this number.

2. Projected Annual Living Expenses at Financial Security or Retirement

If my clients are enjoying their current standard of living and want to maintain it into retirement, I will usually leave the number here the same as number 1. If they are young and haven't reached a desired standard of living yet, then I may increase it. If they are only a few years away from retirement and expect to reduce debt, move and so forth to reduce the expenses of living, then I may reduce it. *Don't get hung up here!* Just pick a number that you think is appropriate for the client's education, location, and so on that represents a good standard of living and go with it. **Another point: This is in today's dollars.**

3. **Number of Years to Financial Security or Retirement**

Self-explanatory. Remember to ask the client when he wants to be financially secure. Financial security and retirement are often two separate goals.

4. **Forecasted Inflation Rate**

Don't be hung up on today's inflation rate. Inflation has been with us for more than 50 years and has averaged about 4 percent. Don't be afraid to use historical averages or to adjust for location. Some will argue that they are not affected as heavily by inflation because they are not buying houses. All true, but who knows whether they may be affected more in some areas of their living expenses and less in others. Don't argue about it. Just ask the client what he thinks his personal rate will be.

5. **Annual Living Expense in Future Dollars**

Using your financial calculator, just convert line 2 to future dollars using the number of years and inflation rate.

6. **Retirement Benefits**

Remember the end result we are looking for: How much money is the client going to have to accumulate to support his desired lifestyle in retirement? If he already has a retirement plan that you have nothing to do with, then you are dealing with a segregated portion of his other assets. If you are also assisting with the retirement plan as to how much to contribute, then you may not want to include it here but include it in the bottom number and segregate the earning assets needed *inside* and *outside* retirement plans.

This was a major hang-up for me if neither the client nor I knew much about the client's retirement plan. How could I forecast this number? I found some rules of thumb that showed the average plan provided about 30 percent of salary at retirement, with the low being 15 percent and a high of 60 percent. If the plan is good, the employee will generally know what he can count on. If it is not, then he won't. A phone call to the company may tell you. To avoid being hung up on this number, I estimate at about 20 to 40 percent, depending on what I know about the company. If the client is contributing to a 401K or similar plan, you can project salaries and values using today's rate of contribution. As for Social Security, I estimate the maximum benefit based on today's maximum benefit of just less than $1,200 per month. If the client is younger than 30, I don't consider Social Security.

7. **Net Annual Income Required from Investments**

Line 5 less line 6. This is the amount the client himself must generate for retirement from investments.

8. **Expected After-Tax Rate of Return**

Use a conservative rate based on a portfolio of diversified investments. I usually use a rate ranging from two to eight points above inflation, depending on the client's risk profile. The higher the risk profile, the higher the rate you can project.

9. **Capital Needed for Retirement**

Line seven divided by line eight. This will tell you the amount of money you will need to have invested to produce the income needed on line seven. I try to avoid projecting a liquidation of capital, because I don't know when the client will die. Sometimes, however, it may be necessary.

10. **Liquidation Proceeds of Investments Not Needed after Retirement**

List all the assets that the client plans to liquidate to fund his retirement. This can have a major impact on the earnings required. For example, if a client intends to sell a highly valued personal residence at retirement and live in an apartment, then the after-tax proceeds would be available to invest in an earning asset.

11. Net Investment (Earning Assets) Needed

Line 9 less line 10. This is what the client will need to accumulate. Now you have a target to aim for. The plan should start to have meaning for you and the client.

Following is a sample worksheet that could be used to determine assets required:

How Much Will You Need?
Financial Security Planning Worksheet

December 1996

John B. & Susie Q. Average

1. Current annual living expense needs	$ 60,000
2. Projected annual living expense at financial security or retirement	50,000
3. Number of years to financial security or retirement	20
4. Forecasted inflation rate	4%
5. Annual living expense in future dollars	$109,556
6. Less retirement benefits, Social Security, corporation retirement	50,000
7. Net annual income required from investment	59,556
8. Expected *after-tax* rate of return	6%
9. Capital needed for retirement	$992,600
10. Less liquidation (after-tax) proceeds of investments not needed after retirement	
1. Personal real estate	—
2. Business real estate	—
3. Business equipment, Goodwill, and so forth	
4. Other	
Subtotal	
11. Net investment (earning assets) needed	$992,600

D. College Education Planning Worksheet

If your client has stated a goal of educating his children, he probably has no idea of the costs he may incur. If he has not stated it as a goal and has minor children, then you need to ask about college funding. This form allows you to highlight for the client the need to plan ahead.

1. Current Four-Year Cost of College

If you don't know this cost,

a. Ask the client if he does

b. Call the college

c. Call your favorite product sponsor

d. Call your regional training center or your Broker-Dealer

2. Number of Years Until College Enrollment

Self-explanatory

3. Forecasted Inflation Rate

College cost inflation has been running well ahead of the national rate. You may want to use a higher percentage here.

4. College Costs in Future Dollars

Inflation rate applied to the current costs for number of years.

5. Less Other Funds Available

If the client has funds set aside already, they should be included here.

6. Net Amount Required for College Funding

You can get more exact here, showing how much is required for year one, year two, three, four, and so on. I think it is a waste of time unless the client requests it. Remember, these are estimates anyway.

7. Monthly Investment Required

Use your financial calculator to calculate the monthly investment required. The rate of return will depend on the client's time horizon and risk tolerance. Most clients will usually tolerate a little bit more risk in a college education fund than in other investments.

Here is a sample worksheet that could be used for college education planning:

How Much Will I Need?
College Education Planning Worksheet

CHILD'S NAME: Jerry Average
DATE: December 1996

1. Current four-year cost of college (room, board, tuition)	$28,000
2. Number of years until college enrollment	9
3. Forecasted inflation rate	6%
4. College costs for four years in future dollars	47,000
5. Less other funds available	0
6. Net amount needed for college funding	47,000
7. Monthly investment required at 8%	297

CHILD'S NAME Holly Average
DATE December 1996

1. Current four-year cost of college (room, board, tuition)	28,000
2. Number of years until college enrollment	11
3. Forecasted inflation rate	6%
4. College costs for four years in future dollars	53,000
5. Less other funds available	0
6. Net amount needed for college funding	53,000
7. Monthly investment required at 8%	250
Total monthly investment required at 12 %	434
Total monthly investment required at 10 %	488
Total monthly investment required at 8 %	547

Step 5: **Estate Values/Liquidity Test**

Total net worth from prior schedule	$259,420
Add: life insurance you own or will purchase	300,000
Total estate value	559,420
Total estimated estate tax due on death of second	
spouse based on today's value of estate	$0

For larger estates, I will use a larger form that not only shows the detail that makes up the estate value, but projects it into the future to some estimated date of death. I will then calculate the current estate tax liability and the projected future liability. I compare this to the amount of liquid assets available to pay such estate taxes. I will first recommend ways to reduce estate taxes. I then calculate the effect of these measures on the estate tax due. If there is still a problem of not having enough liquid assets to pay the taxes, I will recommend some method to solve this liquidity problem. This could involve a buildup or conversion of assets to reach the desired level of liquidity or the purchase of insurance specifically to meet this need.

Since this is a small plan and a client who does not have immediate estate tax or liquidity problems, I did not unduly complicate the plan with estate problems. I will note in the file to follow up at a later date.

Step 6: **Insurance Needs**

A. **Life Insurance Needs Worksheet**

This form is excellent for arriving at a desired level of insurance coverage for your client. It should be understandable to the client.

Line 1. Annual Income Required to Support Family

At this time in the financial plan, you should know what the annual living expense needs are. When one spouse dies, that living expense need may increase or decrease. For example, if a wife who is a homemaker dies, the additional costs for sitters for the children may more than offset her normal expenses for clothing, food, and so forth. As a rule of thumb, I use a 15 percent reduction in living expenses when one spouse dies, which may be adjusted for special circumstances I am aware of.

Line 2. Income Available

This is a total of other income sources available when one spouse dies. Social Security benefits may be available for minor children, the surviving spouse may be able to continue to work or go back to work, and there may be income from other investments. However, do not include income from investments set aside for college or retirement.

Line 4. Capital Base Required to Produce Additional Income

Line three divided by a reasonable rate of expected return. This rate should be conservative.

Line 5. Lump-Sum Requirements

These are the payments that may be required at death. Judgment and client consultation are required here, but you can make some reasonable predictions as to which debts would need to be paid because of the loss of one spouse's income. Funeral and settlement costs vary from state to state, but I use a rate of 8 percent of the estate for such things as probate costs, administrative costs, and funerals.

Line 6. Total Capital Required

Total of lump-sum requirements (bills that must be paid within one year of death) and income requirements.

Line 8. Sale of Other Assets and Assets Available to Meet Liquidity Needs

The client may have assets that will not be retained if one spouse dies. The proceeds from their sale can be used to reduce insurance requirements. Similarly, the client may have assets that can be used to meet lump-sum requirements. For example, education funds can reduce the lump-sum requirements.

Following are two sample Life Insurance Needs Worksheets:

Life Insurance Needs Worksheet

NAME: John B & Susie Q. Average

DATE: December 1996

Husband √   Wife

Annual income required to support family		$51,000
		(1)
Income available		
Social Security	0	
Spouse's income	60,000	
Income from other investments	5,000	
Total income available		65,000
		(2)
Additional income required		
(line 1 minus line 2)	0	
		(3)
Capital base required to produce additional		
income @____% (line 3 ÷ ____ %)		0
		(4)
Lump-sum requirements		
Debt payments	16,000	
Funeral and estate costs	20,000	
Estate taxes	0	
Education costs	100,000	
Other	10,000	
Total lump-sum requirements		146,000
		(5)
Total capital required		146,000
		(6)
Total life insurance in force		50,000
		(7)
Less: Sale of nonearning assets	—	
Assets available to meet liquidity needs	—	0
		(8)
Total additional insurance needed		$96,000
		(9)

Life Insurance Needs Worksheet

NAME: John B & Susie Q. Average
DATE: December 1996
Husband   Wife √

Annual income required to support family		$51,000
		(1)
Income available		
Social Security	0	
Spouse's income	45,000	
Income from other investments	5,000	
Total income available		50,000
		(2)
Additional income required		
(line 1 minus line 2)		1,000
		(3)
Capital base required to produce additional		
income @ 6 % (line 3 ÷ 6 %)		17,000
		(4)
Lump-sum requirements		
Debt payments	16,000	
Funeral and estate costs	20,000	
Estate taxes	0	
Education costs	100,000	
Other	10,000	
Total lump-sum requirements		146,000
		(5)
Total capital required		163,000
		(6)
Total life insurance in force		50,000
		(7)
Less: Sale of nonearning assets	—	
Assets available to meet liquidity needs	—	0
		(8)
Total additional insurance needed		$113,000
		(9)

B. Disability or Income Continuation

The disability worksheet is purposefully kept simple and should be self-explanatory.

Line 1. Total Income Needs

Monthly living expenses should be available from other sections of the plan. Business overhead expenses are applicable if the client has a business that would need to be continued in the event of his short- or long-term disability.

Line 2. Income Available If Disabled

Be sure to determine whether the current coverage is long term or short term. Most corporate benefits policies are short term. Social Security usually has a long-term waiting period to qualify and requires total and permanent disability. Be sure that investment income does not include funds set aside for retirement or other specific purposes such as education funds.

The Disability Needs Worksheet could look like this:

Disability Needs Worksheet

Husband

Total monthly living expenses	$5,000
Business overhead needs (if applicable)	0
Total income needs	5,000 $ (1)

Income available (if disabled)

Current disability coverage	0 $
Social Security (if permanently and totally disabled)	Not Considered $
Spouse's income	5,000 $
Investment income	400 $
	$
	$ (2)
Total income available	5,400 (2)
Additional disability insurance needed (Line 1 minus line 2)	0 $ (3)

(continued)

(*continued*)

Wife

Total monthly living expenses	5,000
Business overhead needs (if applicable)	0
Total income needs	5,000 $ (1)
Income available (if disabled)	
Current disability coverage	0 $
Social Security (if permanently	
and totally disabled)	0 $
Spouse's income	3,750 $
Investment income	400 $
	$
	$ (2)
Total income available	4,150 (2)
Additional disability insurance needed	850 $ (3)
(Line 1 minus line 2)	

Step 7: **Our Recommendations**

This is the "tell them what you told them" part of the plan. I usually try to cover each goal again with specific recommendations to reach each goal. Emphasize advantages of taking the recommended steps. This is the **solution** part of the sale when you are presenting the plan. I also often repeat the funds required for each goal to remind the client where he is trying to go.

The recommendations section might be prepared like this:

Our Recommendations

Goal # 1

To be financially independent at John's age 60 with an annual income of $50,000 stated in today's dollars.

As you can see from the financial security planning worksheet, it will take approximately $109,556 in income to have the same purchasing power as $50,000 in 20 years (John's age 60). Based on information you provided about

(*continued*)

(continued)

your company pension plans, they should provide approximately $50,000 of the amount needed. This leaves $59,556 that will be required from your own investments. At a conservative after-tax rate of return of 6 percent for your retirement years, you need to accumulate an estimated $992,600 to meet your goal. This assumes that you will not spend any of your principal. We don't know how long you both are going to live or what unexpected events may occur between now and retirement age and certainly not after retirement age is reached. Since you want to retire at John's age 60, I do not recommend including any spending of principal until at least his age 75. Accumulating this much principal to meet your goal may require some living adjustments and some aggressive investing strategies, but I believe that reaching your goal is possible.

Based on the data you provided, your current living expenses, including all insurance payments, loan payments, fixed and current obligations, total approximately $60,000 per year. Taxes consume another $20,000. This leaves approximately $25,000 of your total income available to invest toward your goals.

I recommend that you invest by bank draft $1,300 per month ($15,600 per year) toward goal #1. At a growth rate of 10 percent per year average over the 20-year period, you should accumulate approximately $995,000. We should review this plan at least annually to check progress toward your goal. The investments recommended certainly may return more or less than 10 percent, but we can adjust as the need arises. If 10 percent investment performance is not achieved during the initial periods, we can increase the amount of investment as your income changes. You will also have some additional disposable income when your house is paid for in 15 years and when the children finish college. The $1,300 will be distributed as follows:

20% in a domestic small cap aggressive growth mutual fund

30% in a domestic large cap growth fund

(continued)

(continued)

20% in a fund that invests in foreign stocks and bonds

30% in a tax-deferred variable annuity (since you do not have the opportunity to shelter income from taxes through profit sharing plans at your places of employment.)

The variable annuity will be allocated to separate accounts as follows:

50% to growth and income

50% to high-yield bonds

Goal #2

To accumulate enough funds to pay for Jerry and Holly's education at a state university.

Based on the schedules attached, it will cost approximately $47,000 for Jerry's education and $53,000 for Holly's. This is based on a 6 percent inflation rate for college expenses from now until they reach college age. College expenses have been more than double the national inflation for several years, but I do not know how long that trend will continue. As in the case with goal #1, we will review our projections and progress at least annually and make any adjustments required.

I recommend that you open Uniform Transfer to Minor accounts for both children and start investing $275 per month for Jerry and $225 per month for Holly. These investments should be made by bank draft.

At a growth rate of 8 percent per year for their investments, you will need to start investing approximately $547 for both children's future college costs. Because you currently do not have the disposable income to fully fund all of your goals, I recommend a more aggressive strategy to possibly reach returns of 10 to 12 percent and allow $500 per month to achieve your goals. Each of the UTMA accounts will be invested in aggressive growth equity funds. As the children get closer to col-

(continued)

(continued)

lege age, we will start transferring to more conservative investments. When they reach college age, we should have the first year's expenses fully funded in a liquid, low-risk investment such as a money market fund.

Goal #3

To provide funds for weddings for both children.

You are wise to plan for wedding expenses. I have had many clients have to borrow from retirement funds or extend their working years in order to pay for weddings. Based on the type of wedding you described for both children and consultation with a local wedding planner, I estimate that today's cost of the bride's portion of Holly's wedding would be $15,000. You told me that you want to be financially prepared for this when she reached age 22. In 15 years, that same wedding will cost approximately $27,000. The groom's portion of Jerry's wedding as you describe it would cost approximately $5,000 today and $8,000 at his age 22. You can fund both these future happy events with approximately $90 per month. ($65 for Holly and $25 for Jerry). *I recommend that you include these drafts in your education UTMA accounts. We will follow the same strategy for switching to more conservative investments as we come closer to wedding times.*

Goal #4

To protect our assets and income stream to ensure we reach our goals.

You are both to be commended for not only designing a plan to enhance the quality of all family members' lives, but also for taking steps to protect yourselves from unforeseen events. Balancing a family's need to accumulate with the need to protect often creates conflicting goals that compete for limited assets. However, I believe that you can achieve both in your situation. Determining how much insurance a couple

(continued)

(*continued*)

needs is obviously not an exact science. My rule of thumb is not to buy protection for those events that you can afford to pay for out of current assets or earnings. In your particular situation, I took disposable income and subtracted the amount required to fund goals 1 through 3. The remainder will be used to purchase additional protection for your lives and your income streams.

According to the worksheets attached, you need the following additional levels of protection:

Life insurance for John	$ 96,000
Life insurance for Susie	113,000
Disability for Susie	$850 per month income protection

These are estimates only and were calculated using very conservative needs projections.

Although my worksheets do not suggest additional disability protection for John, there would be an undeniable drop in living standards and possibly a substantial increase in living costs if John were to incur certain types of disability. His health insurance and short-term disability provide some protection, but more disability for John will be one of the first things to add to the plan when we review it next time. Right now, we are trying to take positive steps in the direction of your goals; not climb the entire financial mountain in one leap. As for life insurance protection, you may have increasing needs for coverage as the value of your estate grows. For now, *I recommend the following:*

1. *Keep the two $50,000 in permanent coverage that you each currently own.*
2. *Add $100,000 in term insurance for both John and Susie. This insurance will be convertible to permanent without additional physicals. I also recommend riders to allow you to purchase an additional $100,000 each of permanent insurance.*

(*continued*)

(*continued*)

3. *After one year, add additional disability coverage for John.*
4. *After two years, we will look at adding additional disability coverage for Susie.*
5. *After two years, we will also look at life insurance needs again and consider the need for protecting this insurance from estate taxes.*

Goal #5

To build a small house in the country to use as a second home before Susie reaches age 50.
You have informed me that Susie's parents plan on giving you the acreage to build on. You indicated that your goals were stated in order of importance. This goal, therefore, took the last priority. However, I also believe that this goal is very attainable in the time frame mentioned. Based on the house you described, today's construction costs would be approximately $100,000. In eight years, those costs would probably reach $137,000. You currently have $90,495 in investments and cash that have not been considered in reaching any of the other four goals. A certificate of deposit for $78,400 that is currently paying 4.5% that matures next month, $8,453 in mutual funds, and $3,642 in individual stocks. *I recommend the following:*

1. *Cash the CD when it matures and move $40,000 into a money market fund with the same mutual fund family where your retirement investments are being held. This will serve as your emergency fund. It pays 5.2% yield (more than your CD) and is more liquid. Use $4,000 to pay off existing credit card debt. The $34,400 remaining should be invested in the existing account you have in Brand C growth and income fund.*
2. *Sell the individual stock in Go-Go Widget, Inc. You don't have enough shares to actively trade individual stocks.*

(*continued*)

(*continued*)

> The stock is down from your original purchase price and doesn't appear to be headed up soon. Put the proceeds of $3,642 into the same growth and income fund as in #1.
>
> 3. The $46,495* now invested in Brand C growth and income fund should reach $86,059 in eight years at an 8 percent rate of growth.
>
> 4. To make up the difference between $86,059 and $137,000, you can either obtain financing or borrow from your emergency fund. It should have grown to approximately $59,000 by this time.

*$ 8,453 Original Balance
  34,400 Additional Deposit from CD
 +3,642 Sale of Stock
 $46,495

Other Recommendations

This is my reminder sheet to see whether I have covered everything that might apply to this client. If I find something on this list that properly belongs in another part of the plan, I go back and add it in the appropriate place.

Here is a sample list for other recommendations:

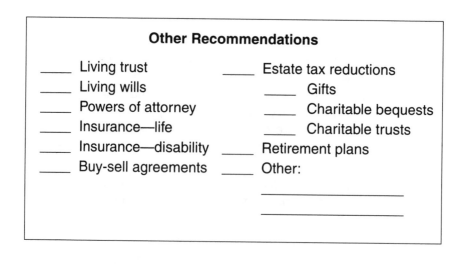

Other Recommendations

_____ Living trust	_____ Estate tax reductions
_____ Living wills	_____ Gifts
_____ Powers of attorney	_____ Charitable bequests
_____ Insurance—life	_____ Charitable trusts
_____ Insurance—disability	_____ Retirement plans
_____ Buy-sell agreements	_____ Other:
	_____
	_____

The implementation sheet is for your internal use. It is a reminder to you and your assistant of the procedural steps to be taken when a client is actually ready to implement his financial plan. These implementation procedures should be done before your meeting with the client and kept in the file for future reference.

The implementation sheet might look like this:

Implementation

1. Prepare bank draft and mutual fund applications to invest $910 per month into brand X mutual fund, allocated as follows:
   a. $260 to aggressive small cap (*name of fund*)
   b. $390 to large cap growth fund (*name of fund*)
   c. $260 to their foreign fund (*name of fund*)
   d. $390 to brand B variable annuity
      (1) Allocate 50% to growth and income account
      (2) Allocate 50% to high-yield bond fund account
2. Set up applications for Uniform Transfer to Minor Accounts for education and wedding funding in brand Y mutual funds for Jerry and Holly. Design bank drafts of $300 per month for Jerry and $290 per month for Holly allocated 100% to *name of aggressive growth fund.*
3. Prepare insurance applications for both Susie and John for $100,000 in convertible term. The insurance should have riders allowing not only conversion, but the purchase of additional insurance of at least $100,000 each within the next ten years. Run illustrations on at least three competing companies and prepare an analysis for my review before meeting with the client.
4. Prepare disability application for Susie requesting $850 per month long-term disability coverage with own occupation coverage. Also run competing illustrations from two companies for my review.
5. Prepare certificate of deposit rollover forms to transfer $40,000 of the proceeds to a money market fund with (*name of mutual fund*). Transfer remainder of $34,400 into client's existing account with C mutual fund company.
6. Prepare stock power forms for selling stock in Go-Go Widgit, Inc. Invest proceeds in C mutual fund in same existing account.

Index

NOTES

NOTES

NOTES

NOTES

NOTES